HUNGRY FOR GOD

An inspirational guide to fasting

BRIAN SAUDER

House To House Publications
Lititz, Pennsylvania USA
www.h2hp.com

Hungry for God
An inspirational guide to fasting

by Brian Sauder

Copyright © 2019

Published by
House to House Publications
11 Toll Gate Road, Lititz, PA 17543 USA
Phone: 717.627.1996
www.h2hp.com

ISBN-13: 978-0-9987574-6-9
ISBN-10: 0-9987574-6-2

Dedication

This book is dedicated to all who have been inspired to fast by this teaching in the past and those who will be inspired in the future. I am rejoicing in all that God has done and will do as we seek Him together.

Acknowledgements

Janet – As my wife you have inspired me to follow my heart at so many crucial times.

Sauder kids – Thanks for letting me sit at the dinner table even though I was not eating. Also…thanks for the content reading of this book.

Larry Kreider – As a mentor and spiritual father you have encouraged me to write, teach and make disciples.

House to House Publications team – Thanks to Sarah Sauder and the team for making this book a possibility. It will change the world.

DOVE International family – Thanks to so many for serving as a sounding board as I experimented and hammered out these truths on fasting.

CONTENTS

Foreword

I have known Brian Sauder for more than forty years and have been privileged to walk alongside him in various areas of leadership. Brian writes this book on fasting from a position of spiritual authority because he lives what he writes. Fasting is not mere theory for Brian. The truths that he shares with conviction and passion have been tested on the anvil of his own personal experience.

I have read many books on prayer and fasting during my years in Christian leadership and ministry. But *Hungry for God* is my favorite book on fasting. It is biblical, practical and written by a true practitioner who practices what he preaches. Fasting has become a lifestyle for Brian. We can experience the same life of victory and breakthrough through the practice of fasting. After all, fasting is not an option for the believer in Christ. It should be a way of life. Jesus said, "When you fast…"

As you read each page of this book, I believe you will receive a fresh hunger for the Lord, for His presence and for His purposes to be fulfilled through your life. Let's expect the Lord to give us fresh revelation and a renewed sense of His presence as we grow in fasting and prayer.

Larry Kreider
DOVE International

Introduction

"Go on a fast for forty days? You have got to be joking! That is impossible! Only super-spiritual, crazy Christians do things like that. I could never do it. I would die. I haven't fasted beyond a few days and now you are asking me to fast for forty days?"

This is exactly what I would have said until I received a revelation about fasting.

Since that time, I have completed ten forty-day fasts and many other shorter fasts with different numbers and themes associated with them. I have seen so many breakthroughs in my life through extended fasting that I am solidly sold on it for myself and for every Christian. Many, many, many times I have heard God's voice and discerned the way to move forward while on extended fasts.

This book contains my incredible story of how the Lord taught me to fast. It also examines many individuals in the Bible who fasted and looks at some key proponents of fasting in church history.

Fasting is like hitting the reset button on your computer. It puts things back in the order God intended. We know that we are spiritual beings but many times we are controlled by the natural desires of our flesh and the battles that go on in our minds. When we fast, it puts our spirits in control and our bodies and souls under the influence of our spirits. It feels so good at the end of an extended fast. Things just feel right.

One of the old time fasting teachers you will meet in this book is Franklin Hall. Franklin would say, "Food abstinence allows man to get closer to the spirit realm than by any other way... Mountains are moved by fasting." In the Bible, mountains often represent strongholds that need to be moved. Nothing is impossible through prayer and fasting.

Jesus taught that there is more power available through prayer and fasting than there is from prayer alone. Fasting is like a multiplier that increases the effectiveness of our prayers. Even though you may have never fasted a day in your life, I invite you to read how the Lord taught me to fast. It is possible and you cannot argue with the results.

CHAPTER ONE

Hungry
for God

> As I have learned to seek the Lord, placing my heart
> and body before Him, my faith has grown and also my
> trust in Him. The emptiness of my stomach has drawn
> my heart to hunger more for His Spirit's provision. I
> am grateful for such a sweet invitation. — Ashley

Are you hungry for God? If your answer is "Yes," it means you want more of His presence and more of His power in your life. You want to know His direction for your career or ministry. Over the last few years, I have met many people who are passionate to follow the Lord. They are ready to do whatever it takes to find His will for their lives and break-through the barriers that would keep them from following Him wholeheartedly.

Is there more available to us as Christians? When Paul was writing to the Ephesian Christians he told them he kept praying that they "would receive a spirit of wisdom and revelation knowledge to know the Father better, know the hope of

His calling and know the riches of His glorious inheritance."[1] Wow! There must be more available.

Hungry for God

Through fasting we can get a glimpse into what the Lord has in store for us. These are the secrets He keeps from just the casual inquirer but makes available to those who want to go deeper in Him. In a great paradox of biblical history, we find Esau despising his birthright and losing part of his natural inheritance when he was physically hungry (Genesis 25:29). We want the opposite—to gain more of our God-given spiritual inheritance by turning our faces toward the Lord through voluntary natural hunger.

Proverbs 16 states, "The laborer's appetite works for him; his hunger drives him on" (16:26). This is true both in the natural and spiritual world. Our appetite for more of the Lord drives us to receive more of what He has for us.

As a believer and minister I was hungry for more of the power of the Lord. I was stirred to read the biography of Mahesh Chavda because I saw God's power being released in his ministry. Mahesh is an Indian man who came to the Lord and has a powerful healing ministry. So, as I was reading in his biography, without any warning he talks about fasting as a source of the spiritual power of God in his life. With shock I read that he completes two forty-day fasts—*and* two twenty-one-day fasts—every year. I couldn't believe it. *That is impossible,* I thought, I had to pick my jaw up from the floor because of the shock. I started to add up days in the year because this seemed like he was *not* eating as often or more often than he *was* eating. I found out it was not actually more days of fasting than eating, but it sure got my attention.

This is when I received the first indication that I should go on a forty-day fast. At this point I had never fasted more than a week in my life. I decided I would go on a forty-day fast. However, it seemed prudent to try a twenty-one-day fast first, just to see if I could do it. In the fall of 1994, I went on my first twenty-one-day fast in fear and trembling. Looking back, I would call it a rather sloppy fast in regards to what I was eating. I liquefied a lot of stuff in the blender to make milkshakes and smoothies that I would not have while on a fast now. However, God met me where I was. The twenty-one-day fast 'worked.' I experienced God in a new and tangible way.

What if we lose our reward?

The next year in 1995 I read Bill Bright's book entitled *The Coming Great Awakening*. In it, Bill tells the story of going on his first forty-day fast at the age of seventy. I learned something that really helped me. Bill said we must talk about fasting more. We should teach it and preach it. We should share stories of the miraculous things that happen when fasting.[1] Obviously he was talking about it publicly as he was writing a book about fasting. One of the great historic proponents of fasting from the 1950's Franklin Hall, said the same thing:

Fasting is a cornerstone of the Christian religion, yet there is seldom, if ever, a complete sermon on the subject. Moreover, it is an important, basic truth of the Bible; yet we so often overlook its value. Fasting is mentioned in the Scriptures approximately one-third as much as prayer, yet our present day church member places it insignificantly in the background.[2]

Understanding this concept helped me because I had always been taught that scriptures indicate we should fast in private and our reward would be given in public. I understood this to mean we should not tell people when we are on a fast, since if we failed to keep it a secret but rather talked about fasting we would lose the reward. This came from a misunderstanding of Matthew 6:16-18.

When you fast, do not look somber as the hypocrites do, for they disfigure their faces to show others they are fasting. Truly I tell you, they have received their reward in full. But when you fast, put oil on your head and wash your face, so that it will not be obvious to others that you are fasting, but only to your Father, who is unseen; and your Father, who sees what is done in secret, will reward you.

As Bill Bright explained in his book, this passage of scripture was teaching that we should not fast as the Pharisees did, that is, to arrogantly call attention to their fasting. The Pharisees would put ashes on their heads and wear sackcloth to proudly draw attention to the fact that they were fasting.

Jesus was teaching us not to boast about fasting. This does not mean we should not talk about it. I have come to believe the fear of "losing our reward" is actually a distortion of scripture from the devil to prevent us from talking and teaching about fasting!

Fasting is one of the most powerful spiritual tools we have available to us. Fasting is a spiritual discipline; it breaks the power of sin and opens up God's will for our lives. So in this book, I am boldly but humbly talking about fasting.

I not only survived my first twenty-one-day fast in 1994, but found it to be spiritually and physically invigorating. In 1995 I went on my first forty-day fast. It was invigorating as well. I noticed a clear increase in the gift of prophecy in my life. Things started to change for me. I knew I would continue fasting.

Since that first forty-day fast I have been on ten forty-day fasts and many other fasts of shorter time periods. We will look at different lengths of a fast in a later chapter. Honestly, I wish I had started fasting earlier in my Christian life.

1. Bill Bright, *The Coming Revival* (Orlando, FL: New Life, 1995)
2. Franklin Hall, *Atomic Power with God Thru Fasting and Prayer* (San Diego, CA: Self published, 1952) Pg. 10

Chapter One Questions

1. How did Esau lose part of his inheritance when he was hungry in Genesis 25:29?

2. When is it okay to talk about fasting? Will we lose our reward when we talk about fasting?

3. How does fasting break the power of sin and open up God's will for our lives?

4. How is it possible to boldly but humbly talk about fasting?

CHAPTER TWO

Humble Yourself
or God Will

> *Fasting is a form of self-chastisement and will prevent numerous sufferings, complications, accidents and other forced discipline from the hand of God.*
> — *Franklin Hall*

Humble yourself or God will. Wow, that seems a little scary. Could it actually be the more we experience voluntary humility through fasting the less we have to experience other methods of the Lord's discipline? Franklin Hall said this is the case.

In Matthew 4:4 the Bible states that man shall not live by bread alone. Fasting is a form of self-chastisement and will prevent numerous sufferings, complications, accidents and other forced discipline from the hand of God. It is a way to escape Israel's suffering in the wilderness.[1]

I have found this to be true, but in a positive way. The more we voluntarily humble ourselves with fasting the less that God has to humble us. After all, the words *humility* and *humiliation* have the same root. Somehow humility seems better.

I remember sitting at a meeting of pastors while on an extended fast. I listened to others talk about the various challenges and issues they were experiencing in their lives and ministries during the time of sharing. Awkwardly, when it was my turn to share, I didn't have any challenges or struggles to talk about. I almost felt like I should apologize for not having something going wrong in my life. But I simply said I was on a fast and that I felt really close to God, I was getting breakthroughs and things were changing almost daily in my life.

Fast sacrificially

The nature of fasting requires dependence on God's power. Fasting must be a sacrifice. We read in Joel 2:12-13 that fasting represents a time of mourning. It is not life as usual. You are giving up something you enjoy to get closer to God. You will feel at times that you do not have enough energy, but ultimately make it through the day. In your weakness, His strength is made perfect (2 Corinthians 12:9). David himself wrote "I humbled myself with fasting" (Psalm 35:13).

It may seem like an odd analogy, but when someone loses a loved one to death there is a period of mourning. Proper mourning actually provides a healthy separation from the departed loved one. When we talk about a fast as a time of mourning, it means our sacrifice provides separation from our carnal desires and sins. At times when someone becomes a Christian without proper mourning or without feeling sorry for the sins that have separated them from God, they find it harder to walk away from those sins and live a life of victory.

When on a fast, mourning causes an appropriate separation from sinful desires and this opens the door for us to be closer to God. The ancient monks would sometimes use the first ten verses of James 4 to pray and seek God. Here it speaks of grieving and mourning as you approach God, humbling yourself so that He will lift you up.

In the beginning of a fast it is common to feel more carnal than spiritual. I have found this to be true in almost every fast I have undertaken. When I start to fast I could be grumpy, irritable, yelling at my kids and saying things to my wife for which I have to later apologize. This always seems so difficult because I feel like I am getting worse instead of better; more carnal rather than more spiritual. However, during this first part of the fast the junk is getting worked out of me. I like to compare myself to a tube of toothpaste and the fast is what is squeezing the tube. Whatever is inside will come out. If I have anger, it will come out. If I have bitterness, it will come out. If I have impatience, it will come out. This is the start of the cleansing process.

The first few days of a fast are usually the most difficult time to even pray. Your prayers seem weak and hollow. Keep praying regardless of how you feel. You must focus on getting through one day at a time; eventually the fast itself actually becomes a prayer, a wordless prayer. When you get over "the hump," it becomes easier; often it even feels like you get stronger physically.

We will talk more about this wordless prayer concept later. A Christian can have such power. Obstacles will seem easier and easier to surmount as they press on.

Hunger leaves

People who get discouraged and quit the fast in the early days never reach the good, joyful and fruitful part of the fast. Franklin Hall says it like this;

> Your will power will be tried until hunger leaves, a few days after the fast begins. Then it is just habit hunger. There will be weakness and discouragement for about 7-10 days. The misery of the fast begins which is a victory over the flesh. The fast is truly a fight and victory is certain if one never gives up. Habit hunger comes at mealtimes. Sometimes pain and cramps in muscles, this is normal. Poisons are working loose in the body.[2]

We will discuss how "hunger leaves" later, but I have found it true that after a certain part of the extended fast you literally do not get hungry anymore. Please bear this in mind when fasting. Great spiritual battles may be fought at certain intervals in a long fast. Sometimes at thirty to forty days, the biggest breakthroughs come. This was true for Jesus. However, the brutal battle of your willpower over weakness and discouragement in the first few days must first be won.

In his book *No Easy Day*, Navy SEAL Mark Owen talks about how he made it through the physically demanding training to be a Navy SEAL. He focused on one day at a time. In many cases, he had to set a goal to just get through part of the day at a time. He would tell himself he could make it to lunchtime, then make it to dinner. That is how it is in the early days of a fast. One day at a time, and sometimes one meal at a time, until it eventually becomes easier. Then God seems closer.

More than just giving up chocolate cake

To get to the point…in this book I am encouraging extended fasting of many days with only juice or water. We are talking about more than just giving up chocolate cake or desserts or an hour of television each day or our favorite social media. Although I believe in partial or media fasts, if we are going to see God miraculously intervene in our lives, ministries and businesses, and hear His voice for major life decisions, it will take serious fasting for days on only juice and water. This is not only my opinion, but also my experience. Having said that, we will discuss a certain type of partial fast called the Daniel fast later in this book. The Daniel fast is a great method groups can use to seek the Lord together over extended periods of time, usually twenty-one days.

Another important thing I learned from Bill Bright's book was to look at II Chronicles 7:14 through the lens of fasting. This often-quoted scripture states,

If my people, who are called by my name, will humble themselves and pray and seek my face and turn from their wicked ways, then I will hear from heaven, and I will forgive their sin and will heal their land.

I have been a part of many pastors' meetings and regional gatherings where this scripture has been referenced and prayed. However, I was curious because it did not seem like our land was getting healing and restored; in fact sometimes it seemed like it was going the opposite direction. Then I read that Bill Bright said there is a level of humility that is only attainable through fasting.

Wow. Maybe this is the missing component from II Chronicles 7:14 that was keeping us from reaching total fulfillment. Dr. Zacharias Fomum agrees, "Those who proudly ask God to heal their land will not be heard. God will normally not heal the land before he forgives the people. He cannot forgive sin that is covered."[3] Fasting bring us to a place of humility that cannot be attained any other way.

1. Franklin Hall, *Atomic Power with God Thru Fasting and Prayer* (San Diego, CA: Self published, 1952) Pg. 52
2. Mark Owan, *No Easy Day* (New York, NY: Penguin Group, 2014)
3. Dr. Zacharias Tannee Fomum, The Ministry of Fasting (New York, NY: Vantage, 1991) Pg. 134

Chapter Two Questions

1. What is voluntary humility?

2. What did David mean when he wrote "I humbled myself with fasting" in Psalm 35:13?

3. Why is it common to feel more carnal than spiritual in the beginning of a fast?

4. What is meant by saying "hunger leaves"?

CHAPTER THREE

A Wordless Prayer

Fasting puts legs to our prayers and gets results that are as powerful as atomic energy. If God's people would only fast 10 days or more there would not be the backsliding, the powerlessness and the lukewarmness in the church. — Franklin Hall (1948)

My goal in this book is to encourage fasting and help make it possible for everyone to fast. The average Christian has to work to feed their family and this makes it difficult to fast and take multiple hours a day in prayer. How do we complete an extended fast if we are not a monk in a monastery somewhere who has nothing to do but pray?

This was the question I asked because I could not take forty days off my job. If we go on an extended fast, shouldn't we be praying many hours each day or all the time? I struggled with this dilemma. The answer came while reading Franklin Hall's thoughts on fasting. He said, "the fast itself actually becomes a prayer...a wordless prayer"[1] for the length of time you are on it. You can still secure very desirable results, and the Lord will bless you, if you can stay in a spirit of prayer while you work. Let me explain.

The fast becomes like a journey you are on with God; the communion you experience with Him over this time is a prayer without words. Understanding that a fast becomes like a wordless 24/7 prayer set me free to fast with great confidence, knowing I was getting the most out of an extended fast. I do pray much more when I am fasting, sometimes specifically dedicating the time slot when I would have been eating to prayer. Also I get other people to pray for me when I am on a fast, especially my small group, pastors and leaders to which I relate.

Understanding fasting as a wordless prayer makes it feel like fasting is something I am doing *with* God and not *for* Him. The fast becomes like a sacrament, similar to baptism or communion: an outward and visible sign of an inward and spiritual experience. I am not fasting to try and get something from God (although I always do receive clear measurable results). Instead, He is realigning my heart; I am changing as well as my circumstances.

Fast silently, but not secretly

I already discussed that we should not be fearful of losing the reward of our fasting by talking about it. We need to give testimonies about the successes and breakthroughs that happen when we are fasting, but without boasting or drawing undo attention to ourselves.

When on an extended fast it is very difficult to keep it a secret. There will always be times when you are around other people over mealtimes. When I first started to fast this presented a problem for me. Since I thought I would lose my reward if I told people about the fast, I would end up saying something that wasn't true like, "I have already eaten" or "I am not hungry." This created another dilemma because now I was lying. So I could either be honest and say I was fasting and "lose my reward," or lie about the fast, which didn't seem to be right either. It was helpful to learn that I could talk about fasting and still not lose my reward.

I have found myself in some interesting discussions with non-Christians as I have been honest about fasting. Once when I was working and we were breaking for lunch, I shared with some work mates that I was not eating because I was on a fast. When they heard it was an extended fast, they responded by asking "Is that for a religious reason?" Of course, I answered "yes" and clarified it was for a spiritual reason to get close to God and hear His voice. That was an interesting lunch break discussion.

When you fast

Sometimes Christians say they do not feel the Lord is leading them to fast or that they will pray about fasting. We have already read the words of Jesus in Matthew 6:16: "When you fast, do not look…" Jesus did not say, "*If* you fast," He said, "*When* you fast." Based on these words of Jesus it does not seem like it is an option for Christians to fast. For every Christian who does not feel "led" to fast or just wants to pray about fasting, this verse is here for you. The Bible introduces fasting as a basic Christian discipline by saying "when" you fast, but does not require a specific length for a fast. This is the part we need to hear from God about—not if we should fast but how long we should fast.

I am recommending regular Spirit-led fasting. Some people will fast a set day a week, for example every Friday, and this works well for them. Though I applaud this approach, it has never worked that well for me. A longer fast of three to forty days helps me focus more, go deeper and get much better results from the time of fasting. So I am regularly asking the Lord to give me an impression about the length and timing of my next fast. Sometimes I go for months and occasionally a year without fasting because I want to follow the Holy Spirit's direction. We will talk more about the lengths of fasts later in the book.

Some may ask if Jesus was supernaturally sustained during the forty-day fast recorded in the Bible. No, this fast was not a supernatural fast. He did it just like we would do it. Fasting is a natural discipline that provides supernatural results. Anyone can fast for long periods of time, but only the Christian can expect supernatural results. The fast of Jesus was natural. After His fast was over, He got hungry. The natural hunger had left His body for a time and returned at the end of the fast. This is generally true in any extended fast; hunger will leave during the fast and return when it is completed.

Be alert and pray

In referencing the end times Peter said we should be alert and pray (1 Peter 3:7). Peter was repeating what Jesus said at the Garden of Gethsemane, "Watch and pray" (Luke 21:36). Maybe this is because Peter himself became sleepy on the Mount of Transfiguration. It seems there is a spirit of slumber that comes on people at critical times, sometimes even during crisis. As Peter and his companions on the Mount of Transfiguration became fully awake, they saw the glory of Jesus (Luke 9:32). Fasting is one way we can battle the spirit of slumber, stay alert and see the glory of Jesus.

The first time I went big game hunting for the white-tailed deer I saw a great example of the kind of alertness that comes when fasting. My hunting mentors told me about the deer's super-sensitive hearing and ability to hear even the slightest sounds in the woods. On the first day of hunting I observed this. I was standing in the woods when a deer came sneaking along. As the deer got closer I realized it was not legal to shoot but also knew the best way to learn about the habits of deer was to watch them in the woods. Every rifle has a safety on it that needs to be released before the gun can be shot. As I watched the deer approach, I slipped the safety off my gun. It made an ever so slight metallic "ping" as it was released. The deer, thirty yards from me, instantly stopped and looked directly at me. Its super-alert ears had picked up this ever so slight sound in the quiet woods.

This is what it feels like for me when I am on a fast. My spiritual ears are supersensitive to what God is saying and it is easier to hear His voice and direction. It seems like the clutter and noise of life are eliminated and I can hear His voice better than I usually can. In the same way a deer can hear even the quietest noise at great distances in the woods, a person on a fast has an increased ability to hear the voice of God. Fasting helps us to be fully awake and feeds into an alert spirit, alert to hear what the Holy Spirit is saying.

An extended fast is an extremely healthy experience and obviously you will lose weight when not eating. On some of my early fasts I would weigh myself each day to see how much weight I was losing. I could say I was trying to monitor my health but more likely it was my vanity in wanting to lose weight. Weighing myself everyday made the fast seem more like a diet than a spiritual experience with God. I soon stopped weighing myself while fasting, except on the first and last day of the fast. This eliminated the distraction of feeling like I was on a diet so that I could focus and humbly seek the Lord and allow Him to change me.

1. Franklin Hall, *The Fasting Prayer* (San Diego, CA: Self published, 1952) Pg 38

Chapter Three Questions

1. Franklin Hall said, "The fast itself actually becomes a prayer...a wordless prayer." What does this mean?

2. How can you fast silently but not secretly?

3. In Matthew 6:16 Jesus is talking about fasting. He said, "When you fast, do not look..." What does this mean for Christians today?

4. How does fasting help you keep Peter's encouragement to be alert and pray (1 Peter 3:7)?

CHAPTER FOUR

Fasting
Changes You

> I heard the teaching on fasting during my internship at a local House of Prayer. Many things hit me including the simple truth in Matthew 6:16 where Jesus clarifies "When you fast..." I was convicted that fasting is essential. — Ashley

As we discussed in the last chapter, Ashley learned fasting is not an option for Christians. Jesus said, "When you fast," knowing that fasting would open up a whole new realm of revelation for believers and make it easier for them to hear the Holy Spirit. In addition to increasing our capacity to receive from the Lord, fasting has a way of quieting all the background noise of life so we can tune in to His voice.

Fasting stretches the wineskins for new wine

When Jesus said that new wine needs new wineskins, He was answering a question from His disciples about fasting. This is important to understand:

They said to him, "John's disciples often fast and pray, and so do the disciples of the Pharisees, but yours go on eating and drinking." Jesus answered, "Can you make the friends of the bridegroom fast while he is with them? But the time will come when the bridegroom will be taken from them; in those days they will fast." He told them this parable: "No one tears a piece out of a new garment to patch an old one. Otherwise, they will have torn the new garment, and the patch from the new will not match the old. And no one pours new wine into old wineskins. Otherwise, the new wine will burst the skins; the wine will run out and the wineskins will be ruined. No, new wine must be poured into new wineskins. And no one after drinking old wine wants the new, for they say, 'The old is better'" (Luke 5:33-39).

The new wine Jesus spoke about is the fresh revelation, insight and direction that we can receive as we, the wineskins, are changed. An extended fast will stretch us and increase our capacity to receive more from God.

The Pharisees asked Jesus why His disciples were not fasting. His response was that there would be a time after He ascended to be with the Father that the disciples would fast. That time to fast is now.

We are the wineskins that need stretching so we can contain new wine. Fasting changes us. Many times I have humbly repented of a critical spirit while fasting. One time it was regarding a co-worker with whom I did not see eye to eye. Under the spotlight of the Holy Spirit, and energized by fasting, something I had been satisfied to call a personality difference was exposed as a critical spirit from which I needed to repent.

Often as I fast I receive revelation to release critical judgments I have made of others. My wife and I own rental properties and rent out apartments. Many of the tenants live on a limited budget and sometimes are late in making payments. It is easy to judge them and how they handle finances. On a recent fast I was challenged by the Lord to release critical judgments against the poor. This even came with a proverb and helped me get the right attitude toward those who were renting from us.

Fasting breaks the critical spirit. Isaiah 58:9 says it like this: "Then you will call, and the Lord will answer; you will cry for help, and he will say: 'Here am I.' If you do away with the yoke of oppression, with the pointing finger and malicious talk..."

One time I was praying for one of my children to be accepted on a certain sports team. While fasting God showed me that the way I was praying was an attempt to exercise a wrong kind of spiritual control over the coach and that I should stop. He was teaching me how to use the authority He has given me in a godly way. If I would release the coach of my controlling prayers, I would gain more authority and be able to use it in a much more significant battle.

Fasting brings a change of heart

I served in an elected government office for nine years. In the public arena there are often political disputes and disagreements that can turn personal and nasty. After one very difficult public situation involving members of our community and the media I was feeling wounded and taken advantage of. While on an extended fast, I received a word from the Lord that broke through this wounding in my life.

God spoke to me about soldiers who are wounded in battle and receive the Purple Heart as a medal to wear. They are awarded this medal to honor their sacrifice in battle. Of course they wear it proudly and this is appropriate. What the Lord indicated to me was that I was wearing my emotional woundedness like a Purple Heart medal and I was proud of it. He spoke to me that if I would give up the pride in my woundedness He would replace the Purple Heart with a heart of gold. In a matter of minutes all the hurt from this experience was gone and the Lord gave me a pure heart toward the involved parties.

How to be holy

God changes us, the wineskins, so we can receive new wine. Fasting brings the revelation that we need to change, and sometimes it is transformational revelation.

For a period of time I had been asking the Lord about how to walk the fine line between holiness and legalism. I found a pattern in my life where I would experience personal revivals and desire to consecrate myself to follow the Lord. However months later I would find myself with just a bunch of religious rules I had made up that didn't have life in them anymore. My desire for holiness had turned into dead legalism.

How could I be holy without falling into legalism? It was during a season of seeking the Lord through fasting that I received the "missing piece" of scriptural insight I needed. God showed me how to live in "up to the minute" holiness without following dead, self inflicted rules. I am now quite confident that God has given me the revelation of how to walk in victory in this area of my life.

Enjoy the fruit of the fast

Sometimes people ask me if I always enjoy fasting. I usually respond by talking about my hobby of running. I run a few times a week or, if possible, every other day. Do I always enjoy every lap around the track or every marker I pass? No. In fact during some laps I wonder if I will make it around that track another time. But I always, always, always enjoy the way I feel after I have finished my run and am sitting, sipping a Gatorade.

I would say the same for fasting. Do I always enjoy every single day of the fast? No. Some days are better than others. But I always, always, always enjoy the way I feel physically, spiritually, mentally and emotionally after I have completed the fast. And I always enjoy the breakthroughs and direction I receive from the Lord.

Most days on a fast are invigorating and energizing. In fact, sometimes when I am nearing the completion of an extended fast I have a sense of disappointment that this time of incredible closeness to the Lord will soon be over and I will start to eat again. However this feeling usually leaves as soon as I start eating. Fortunately the spiritual ground of revelation and breakthrough gained during fasting is maintained long after the fast is complete.

Chapter Four Questions

1. When Jesus was talking about new wineskins, what was He literally talking about? What does it mean for us today?

2. How can a fast help break a critical spirit? (Isaiah 58:9)

3. Fasting can bring the revelation that we need to change. How can we embrace this?

4. What should we do if not every day of our fast is exciting and exhilarating?

CHAPTER FIVE

The Missing Piece
of the Puzzle

> *When you need God's direction, when you are confused about which way to go, one of the best things you can do is fast.*[1] — *Mahesh Chavda*

I love the story of Daniel. He had fasted for a period of three weeks when an angel appeared to him and said, "Since the first day that you set your mind to gain understanding…I have come in response….I have come to explain to you what will happen…" (Daniel 10:12-14). Daniel was asking the Lord a question, and the answer came as he was fasting. I sometimes like to call this the "missing piece of the puzzle." God showed Moses the pattern for the tabernacle on the mountain during fasting. The Bible is full of examples of godly men and women who received direction from the Lord as a result of fasting.

In Acts 13, we find the early church receiving direction from the Lord as they were fasting. In Antioch there was a group of church leaders who were worshiping the Lord and fasting when the Holy Spirit spoke to them about commissioning Barnabas and Paul and sending them on a trip to preach the gospel. This trip later became known as Paul's first missionary journey that took Christianity to areas that previously had not heard the gospel.

On this trip, Paul and Barnabas experienced many miracles, saw many new converts and planted new churches. When it was time to appoint leaders for those churches, how do you think they heard from God about who the leaders should be? It was through prayer and fasting. Leadership selection is a major decision in a church. If fasting should be involved in major decisions in the church, then it should certainly be involved in major decisions in our lives. If you are considering marriage, changing jobs, changing careers, starting a business or other major life decisions it is to your advantage to include fasting in your decision-making process. It will quiet the noise so you can hear clearly.

Listen to Brittany's fasting story...

I had fasted about things in my life on and off, but after hearing some other people's testimonies about longer fasts for a specific area that needed breakthrough, I felt the Lord also call me into a longer fast.

Nine years before my fast, I asked the Lord that I would not date any man other than my husband. Over those nine years, there were many ups and downs and I asked the Lord many times why He had not yet sent my husband.

During the fall of 2013, I felt the Lord call me into a fast between two friend's weddings, both of whom had miracle marriage stories of God bringing them together. The fast was approximately thirty to forty days in length and I decided to do a Daniel's fast.

About two weeks before my fast ended, a man six years younger than me showed interest in a relationship. A series of God-inspired events took place, and we married approximately one year after the first time we got together to talk (me not knowing that this man was already praying about me).

Fasting has been so important in my life. No matter how small or big a request or prayer I have had, God is faithful. Fasting for His promises and answers in our lives is vital to our walk with Him.

Brittany experienced a significant milestone in her life after following the Lord's direction to fast. Her obedience opened the door. There is no scriptural promise that we will find someone to marry or even get what we want by fasting. In fact, sometimes on a fast the Lord will change our desires. But obedience to the Lord in fasting will open the door for Him to do great things.

Sometimes, like Daniel, we are seeking the answer to a question. It happened in the Bible so it is possible for us. Paul was fasting when God called him and gave him the assignment for his life (Acts 9:7-9). Fasting prepares the way for God to give you fresh revelation, fresh vision, and a clear purpose.

Listen to Ashley's fasting story:

God impressed it upon my heart to do my first Daniel fast. Within this time, I had a potential job in Haiti. My faith was bolstered from seeking God the previous year for job direction and I laid this request before Him to give an answer during my fast. During the last forty-eight hours, I started backing down because I had not heard His clear direction yet. Within two hours of the end of my Daniel fast, the director of the school in Haiti sent me a contract!

One young person said this:

I was in a prayer internship that included regular fasting. I was in the middle of making a decision between taking a job in Dubai or at a local women's ministry. Within the first hours of a three-day fast, I received news that made the decision crystal clear: it was the women's ministry!

Is it coincidence that this news just happened to come on the first day of a fast? I don't think so. I have seen so many things happen and change while on fasts that I have come to expect it.

This is the experience of Ezra as well:

Then I proclaimed a fast there at the river of Ahava, that we might humble ourselves before God, to seek from Him the right way for us, and our little ones and our possessions. For I was ashamed to ask of the king for an escort of soldiers and horseman to help us against the enemy on the road, because we had spoken to the king saying, 'the hand of our God is on all those for good who seek Him, but His power and wrath are on all those who forsake Him.' So we fasted and entreated our God for this, and he answered our prayer (Ezra 8:21-23, NKJV).

Ezra was seeking the right way to go and God answered him. But you might ask: *What if I fast and the Lord does not speak to me in a significant way?* This is the wrong question. *What if you fast and He does speak to you?* We know it is His will for us to fast, so we can trust that He will honor our obedience as we seek His voice through prayer and fasting. We will hear His voice and see supernatural things happen.

1. Mahesh Chavda, *The Hidden Power of Prayer and Fasting* (Shippensburg, PA: Destiny Image, 1998) Pg. 58

Chapter Five Questions

1. What does "the missing piece of the puzzle" refer to?

2. How was fasting involved in what became known as Paul's first missionary journey?

3. How did God answer Ezra's prayer as they fasted in Ezra 8:21-23?

4. What revelation did Peter get on the rooftop while fasting in Acts 10?

CHAPTER SIX

Fasting is the Doorway to the Supernatural

> *Food abstinence allows man to get closer to the spirit realm than by any other way.* — Franklin Hall

Fasting is the doorway to the supernatural. It was the same for Jesus. It was after Jesus was fasting in the desert for forty days that He returned and did His first miracle (John 2:11). Jesus turned the water in to wine, and the rest is history. We should expect revelations, dreams and visions when we are on extended fasts. Franklin Hall said, "Food abstinence allows man to get closer to the spirit realm than by any other way."[1] Fasting allows our spirits to connect with God as our physical bodies comes under the influence of the human spirit. When fasting, our human spirits have the opportunity to connect with the Holy Spirit in an entirely new way.

I learned a lot about fasting from Dr. Zacharias Fomum. He was an amazing man from Cameroon. He was known as a scientist, pastor and a prolific teacher and writer. By the end of his life in 2009, he had written more than one hundred scientific publications in international journals and over one hundred books on Christian discipleship, growth, and maturity, with a special emphasis on prayer and fasting. He believed prayer and fasting to be the most vital tool and weapon for the church today. He talks about the release of the supernatural during and after times of fasting like this:

> Many believers have known unusual visitations from the Lord during fasts. The glory of the Lord overshadowed them and they were caught up in the Lord's presence. They were overwhelmed with his presence and it made any pain they felt disappear. Others saw visions of things to come. Others heard the Lord's voice. Some received miraculous healing while to some new spiritual gifts were opened up.[2]

World renowned healing evangelist T.L. Osborne started his amazing healing ministry after going on a forty-day fast. Here are excerpts from a letter he wrote to fasting proponent and author Franklin Hall in 1929:

> (As given to Franklin Hall while visiting with Brother and Sister Osborne in their new house trailer during their wonderful tent cathedral campaign in Reading, Pennsylvania, where three thousand souls found Jesus as their savior and many hundreds were healed from all manner of diseases. Thousands were packed around the tent.) "We were happy to let you know that we feel our lives have been revolutionized by fasting and prayer to Jesus. It was by reading your books that we were enabled to go in to many days and

weeks of fasting and prayer. Both my wife and I have had many deep fasting and prayer experiences. My life was so changed that God began to use me in the healing ministry. As I began to exercise the ministry of praying for the sick, more and more folks were healed.

"One day while in a deep consecration the Spirit spoke thus: 'My son, as I was with Price, Wigglesworth and others, so I will be with thee. They are dead, but now it is time for you to arise and go and do likewise. You can cast out devils, *You* can heal the sick. *You* raise the dead; *you* cleanse the lepers. Behold I give you power over all the power of thee enemy. Be not afraid. Be strong. Be of good courage. I am with thee as I was with them. No evil power shall be able to stand before *thee* all the days of the thy life, as you get the people to believe my Word. I used those men in their day; now I desire to use *thee.'*

"The challenge of this commission, given directly from the Lord, caused me to tremble exceedingly, but I knew God meant every word He had spoken. More days and weeks of fasting and prayer followed this tremendous commission, and many more healings and miracles were the result. We have been able to hold healing campaigns in already over a dozen of our states and on the island of Jamaica, B. W. I. In a single campaign, which we conducted, we saw 125 deaf mutes [healed], ninety totally blind [healed], and hundreds of other equally miraculous deliverances have resulted. Happy and joyful conversions have numbered as many as nine thousand in one revival.

"Brother Hall, we wanted you to know, we do appreciate your vision, and the tremendous way you have stirred the world with fasting and prayer."[3]

Wow. I live thirty minutes from Reading, Pennsylvania where this letter was delivered. There is an indisputable link between prayer and fasting and the supernatural in church history. We see evidence of this from the early apostles to more modern times. Osborne's story was indicative of what was happening at his time.

In 1946 and 1947 a great movement of fasting and prayer was spawned, first in America and then the rest of the world. Franklin Hall's book *Atomic Power With God Through Fasting and Prayer* was the spark that ignited the hearts of thousands to go on extended fasts, seeking God for revival and the restoration of spiritual gifts to the church. He compared the power available through fasting to the power of a nuclear explosion. This was right about the time the atom was split and a nuclear bomb was discovered.

Following its publication, many aspiring evangelists read this book and went on forty-day fasts and subsequently started healing ministries. In 1947 to 1952 the great healing revival broke out through the ministries of Gordan Lindsay, Oral Roberts, T. L. Osborne and a host of others who began to experience gifts of the Holy Spirit. They began to see extraordinary miracles in their ministries and thousands were converted and healed. They were notable because they held their meetings in tents. Most of these itinerant evangelists followed Hall's practice of fasting. Church historians refer to this time as the Healing Revival of 1947 to 1952. But there was more.

In 1948 the "Latter Rain" outpouring visited a Bible college in North Battleford, Canada, and swept into the United States. The leaders all agreed that it was after reading *Atomic Power With God Through Fasting and Prayer* that they entered a season of the "grace of fasting" which, after three months, resulted in a powerful outpouring as the Spirit restored spiritual gifts and ministries to the church. It also led them into employing the laying on of hands for healing and for imparting the gift of the Holy Spirit. The truth of fasting with prayer was a major catalyst in this revival.

The New Testament is filled with many examples of the apostle Paul performing signs and wonders. Where did this power come from? He was a man who practiced fasting. Paul states, "I have known hunger and thirst and have often gone without food" (2 Corinthians 11:27). This same supernatural power to perform signs and wonders that Paul had is available to us.

Mahesh Chavda tells the story of raising a boy from the dead at a massive crusade in 1985 in Zaire:

It was during the outreach in Zaire, that the Lord gave me an unsettling and very specific word of knowledge during one of the meetings..." There is a man here whose son died this morning. Call him up. This day I am going to resurrect his son.!" ...I will never forget the sight of the man running up to the front. Nor will I forget how I felt in that moment, for I knew there was no way I could raise that boy from the dead. Only God could restore life and breath to that man's son... The boy had died at 4:00 a.m. that day from cerebral malaria. By 12:00 noon the six-year-old body of Katshinyi sneezed twice and rose up. God had miraculously raised him from the dead.[4]

A death certificate has been included in one of Mahesh's books to substantiate the miracle. He states, "Coincidentally, I had just completed a forty-day fast prior to this trip to Zaire."

The Bible says it is godly to seek the gifts and supernatural power of God. However we need to let God be God. We should be careful about what we expect from Him as we are seeking Him with prayer and fasting. Sometimes we might be looking for a certain supernatural experience but the Lord wants to give us different one. God wants us to be hungry to experience His power—but He still wants to be God. We can know for sure that He wants to bring spiritual breakthrough in our lives.

1. Dr. Zacharias Tannee Fomum, The Ministry of Fasting (New York, NY: Vantage, 1991) Pg. 129
2. Franklin Hall, *Atomic Power with God Thru Fasting and Prayer* (San Diego, CA: Self published, 1952) Pg. 2
3. Mahesh Chavda, *Only Love Can Make a Miracle* (Ann Arbor, MI:Vine Books, 1990)
4. Mahesh Chavda, *The Hidden Power of Prayer and Fasting* (Shippensburg, PA: Destiny Image, 1998) Pg. 91-92

Chapter Six Questions

1. What are some examples of fasting connected to the supernatural?

2. How did world-renowned healing evangelist T. L. Osborne get started in his healing ministry?

3. The New Testament is full of examples of Apostle Paul performing signs and wonders. According to 2 Corinthians 11:27, where did this power come from?

4. When we are fasting we should be careful about what we expect from God. Why is this?

CHAPTER SEVEN

Fasting for Breakthrough

> *Not knowing anything about fasting I had no idea what to expect. On the morning I started my mom told me my cousin just had surgery about a month ago, was in incredible pain and was unable to walk since then. I decided to pray for him during the fast. Amazingly enough, a week later we received a report that the pain was gone and he was walking. I just about broke down in tears realizing how great our God is to listen to our prayers and hear our cries. I will never forget that moment. It changed my life and how I view prayer and fasting. — Kurtis*

Amazing. I have experienced so many breakthroughs during my times of fasting. It is hard to imagine my life without the breakthroughs in which God intervened in my personal life, ministry, finances, relationships, and more. This book is full of the stories of God's victories in my life and the lives of others. God is the God of the breakthrough.

Mahesh Chavda says it like this, "Fasting is found through-out the Bible. It always seems to show up when ordinary people need extraordinary power, provision and perseverance to overcome impossible odds, enemies or obstructions."[1] But where does this term *breakthrough* originate?

Let's look at the verses from which we get the term "break-through." It is found in I Chronicles 14:8-12:

> When the Philistines heard that David had been anointed king over all Israel, all the Philistines went up to search for David. But David heard of it and went out against them. Now the Philistines had come and made a raid in the Valley of Rephaim. And David inquired of God, "Shall I go up against the Philistines? Will you give them into my hand?" And the Lord said to him, "Go up, and I will give them into your hand." And he went up to Baal-perazim, and David struck them down there. **And David said, "God has broken through my enemies by my hand, like a bursting flood."** Therefore the name of that place is called Baal-perazim. And they left their gods there, and David gave command, and they were burned (ESV).

After this victory, the first thing David did was to rename the valley Baal Perizim, which means "master of break-through," or as we would say today, "Lord of the breakthrough." David describes the victory like "the breakthrough of water." Bible scholars suggest that David's forces probably charged down the slopes of Mount Perazim, like a mountain torrent, sweeping all before them. The force with which God broke through the army of the Philistines is compared with a flood burst its way through all obstacles. David gave all the credit to the Lord.

The Bible is full of examples of leaders fasting and crying out to the Lord for breakthrough. When Jehoshaphat learned he was facing a multitude of Moabites, Ammonites and Meunites in battle, he set himself to seek the Lord and proclaimed a fast for all Judah. He did not fast alone but called a corporate fast. God finds it difficult to turn a deaf ear to fasting. The answer with clear, strategic direction came through the prophet Jahaziel. With God's help, Jehoshaphat routed his enemies (2 Chronicles 20:1-27). Although the victory had been promised, Jehoshaphat still had to face the enemy. From this, we learn that sometimes the end of the fast is not the end of the battle.

This was true for Esther as well. Esther was the one who held the key to breakthrough for the deliverance of her people. Her cousin Mordechai found out about Haman's evil intentions to kill all the Jews. He told her what Haman was plotting and asked her to go to the king on the Jews' behalf. Esther was afraid. She hadn't been allowed to see the king for a month. In fact, no one could see him without being invited. But she fasted and prayed for three days, mustered up her courage and went to see the king. Although he was initially angry at her, the king gave her audience and as events unfolded she was able to see her people saved. Even after she fasted, she still had to take the risk of going in to see the king (Esther 4-6).

A lot of times the results of fasting occur after the fast is completed. We call this *lag*. I experienced this in 2002. I fasted in July of 2002 for a week and believed the Lord had supernaturally given me the scripture Isaiah 9:4, "For as in the day of Midian's defeat, you have shattered the yoke that burdens them, the bar across their shoulders, the rod of their oppressor." This scripture is generally considered to be speaking about the anointing of God (divine empowerment) to break through the yokes of bondage. I received this promise not knowing how I would see it play out. It turned out to be dramatic.

In October of 2002 a sniper called the Beltway Sniper coordinated a series of shootings on the Washington, DC beltway. Ten people were killed and three others injured in locations on the highway around the DC Metro area over three weeks. The whole area was paralyzed with fear and under heavy oppression. Schools closed and many people would not leave their homes. Many in the USA were praying for breakthrough to this horrific assault by the sniper. [1]

Our DOVE International staff met on October 15, and we prayed about this situation. As we prayed I felt the Lord asking me to pray that the sniper would confess his sin. Although this seemed like an odd thing to pray for this murderous individual, I felt the Lord prompt me to pray along these lines. I prayed for the shooter to confess.

I was astonished to find out that a few days later on October 19 the sniper called a Catholic priest and confessed his sin of the DC murders and an additional unsolved murder in Alabama. One source said the caller actually "left his remarks on the priest's answering machine."[2] Why he would do such a thing remains a mystery. The priest contacted the FBI hotline and by Sunday night October 21, the sniper task force was in action. This tip led to the apprehending of the sniper and his accomplice. Of course many millions were praying so I do not want to take credit, but I did simply follow the anointing in prayer and at least contributed to the breakthrough.

God wants to bring breakthrough in even the small practical areas of our lives. In 1997 I was on a forty-day fast praying for lofty things like revival and spiritual awakening among the nations of the world. At the same time my wife and I were experiencing struggles with our young family. To be specific we had a toddler who was not "getting" the idea of potty training and a baby who would not sleep through the night. So while I was fasting for spiritual things like impacting the nations, we were having very practical challenges at home. One day while on this fast I told the Lord, "If You can change the nations, You can certainly help us at home." I added our toddler and baby to my prayer list. My wife is my witness that within one day our toddler was potty trained and our baby was sleeping through the night. Now that is breakthrough!

Increased results in ministry

As the testimony Kurtis reported at the beginning of this chapter demonstrates, fasting often releases physical healing. It was on the first day of a fast in 1999 that I prayed for a lady who was sick and she was immediately healed. In the fall of 2015, I was on a three-day fast focusing on healing for several pastors I knew who were sick. At the same time a good friend of ours had a serious kidney infection and was in the hospital for weeks. He almost died and was told he would be on kidney dialysis for the rest of his life. I drove a few hours to the hospital and prayed for him. Of course I spoke long life and freedom from dialysis over him. Amazingly, within one day the doctors removed the dialysis tubes and talked about sending him home from the hospital. Later I learned that one pastor I was praying for was cleared of cancer. Would all these have happened if I were not fasting? I don't know—but I am going to keep fasting.

During a forty-day fast in 2002, I spoke at a local youth ministry about knowing and achieving your calling. At this meeting over one hundred young people responded to the altar call for more of God and two people gave their lives to Christ. That same night I prayed for a young man's back and he received instant healing. I also prayed with a local businessman because his business was struggling. Later I found out the business was prosperous. Needless to say, I plan to keep on fasting.

1. Mahesh Chavda Quotes, GoodReads.com.
2. *Call to Police Cracks Sniper Case* by Joel Roberts, CBS News, October 24, 2002

Chapter Seven Questions

1. Where does the term "breakthrough" originate in the Bible?

2. When Jehoshaphat learned he was facing a multitude of Moabites, Ammonites and Meunites in battle he set himself to seek the Lord and proclaimed a fast for all of Judah. What happened?

3. Esther held the key to breakthrough for the deliverance of her people. When and how long did she fast?

4. God wants to bring breakthrough in even the practical areas of our lives. List some small, practical breakthroughs you desire to experience in your life.

CHAPTER EIGHT

More Fasting...
More Breakthrough!

> *Fasting begets prophets and strengthens strong men.*
> *Fasting makes lawgivers wise; it is the soul's safe-*
> *guard, the body's trusted comrade, the armor of a*
> *champion, the training of the athlete.*
> — *Basil, Bishop of Caesarea (AD 330-379)*

Breakthrough direction from the Lord

Direction from the Lord is one type of breakthough that might come to us while fasting. Jentezen Franklin states, "When you eliminate food from your diet for a number of days, your spirit becomes uncluttered by the things of the world and amazingly sensitive to the things of God."[1]

When the Lord wanted to advance the kingdom from the Jews to the Gentiles, fasting was a central part of it. Spiritual hunger stirred in the heart of one of the key players, Cornelius, a Gentile centurion in Caesarea who fasted, prayed to God always, and gave generously to the poor (Acts 10:4). God next added Peter to the mix, who was nearby in Joppa. Peter was fasting at that time as well. As Peter shared the gospel with those of Cornelius' household, the Holy Spirit fell and baptized them all. Later they were baptized in water. This was the first time the gospel was available to the Gentiles and one of the greatest breakthroughs in Christian church history. When a person is hungry for God, who knows what is possible.

One time I was fasting and feeling overwhelmed by my busy schedule. I was asking the Lord for direction. As I listened, it became clear that a specific ministry I was overseeing was the one thing I needed to remove from my responsibilities. Just like God's voice...specific and clear. So I took steps to release my responsibility for this ministry to others.

Many times leaders in DOVE International have heard the voice of God in a significant way while engaged in a season of fasting. Larry Kreider, who gets numerous invitations for speaking engagements, often makes the decision about which ones to accept or decline while fasting. All the invitations seem so good, but which are the ones the Lord wants him to take? It is especially important for him to know God's will clearly when extensive travel is involved.

Breakthrough in relational divisions

How about relational breakthroughs? As stated previously, the Scriptures teach in Isaiah 58:9 that fasting will prevent needless divisions. When people are fasting, the heightened discernment allows for recognition of those who might potentially be divisive or offended. This allows for reconciliation, often before any issues have a chance to fester and cause relational damage.

While fasting in 2005 I had a breakthrough conversation with a church leader in Canada who was previously not open to taking input or correction. He shared with me that he had identified an independent spirit in his life and it was affecting the church. He wanted to confess the independent spirit and be free of it. In this situation God brought breakthrough in a leader's attitude and the entire church reaped the benefits. So much happens when I am fasting that it makes me wonder if these things would happen if I were not fasting. My response is that I do not want to take that chance.

Breakthrough in healing

One significant breakthrough for me was in praying for the sick. As we will discuss later, I recommend having a focus for each fast. The more specific the focus the better results. While fasting I have at different times prayed for an increased manifestation of healing when I pray for the sick. As I mentioned, the first time I did this I prayed for a woman who was healed on the first day of the fast. This was a significant confirmation.

Another time it was healing for me personally. I went to the doctor for a physical when I turned age thirty as is recommended. Later the doctor's office called back and said I should return to the office immediately because my thyroid was not functioning properly. I needed to come to pick up a prescription for medication that I would be on every day for the rest of my life. This idea did not sound like God's plan for me. Fortunately, I was planning to start a forty-day fast in just a few days so I told the receptionist I wanted to pray about the thyroid problem and I would like another blood test after the fast. On that fast I continually prayed for the healing of my thyroid. The blood test after the fast showed proper function with no need for medication. Yeah, God!

Opportunity

Many times the breakthrough during fasting is in the form of open doors of opportunity. On one forty-day fast I was on a trip to Canada and over a few days I unexpectedly had the opportunity to pray for a candidate for the Canadian Parliament, pray for a sitting Member of Parliament and meet yet another national Canadian leader whom I won't mention by name.

As I was praying for the Member of Parliament I felt an impression to encourage him that he was like William Wilberforce, the historic English parliamentarian who led the way to the outlawing of slave ownership in England. After we were done praying, he remarked that William Wilberforce was a childhood hero of his and that part of his life dream was to emulate Wilberforce.

I have learned that opportunities that come my way while I am fasting are almost always from the Lord. Once while on a fast, a business leader asked me to coach him in his business.

That request developed into a very fruitful long-standing relationship. Another time a young leader asked me and an associate to be his spiritual mentors as he was leading a growing movement of leaders and churches. My answer was "yes."

Another time we were drilling a new water well for a house we were building while I was on a fast. It was located along the top of a ridge and the area had a history of low-performing wells. As the date for drilling was approaching, in my Bible reading I "happened" to read Deuteronomy 3:13, "About Joseph he said: 'May the LORD bless his land with the precious dew from heaven above and with the deep waters that lie below.'"

"Deep waters that lie below"...wow! That was what we needed. I spoke this verse over our well and sure enough the drilling released an abundant flow of water, much more than what we needed.

Financial breakthrough

Oddly enough, I sometimes receive a significant financial breakthrough on the first day of a fast. I don't know why; maybe this is the Lord just confirming my decision to fast.

One of the ways I receive income is from honorariums when I speak at conferences or churches. It was in November of 2013 and I had just started a seven-day fast when I received one of my largest honorariums for speaking. Along with this honorarium came a contract to coach a business leader for a set dollar amount each month. The chapter following this one is all about financial breakthrough. I know it will help you.

The thoughts of Mahesh Chavda drive home this concept of fasting bringing breakthrough. He says, "Fasting is deeply embedded in God's Word. It is a tool of overcoming leaders in both Old and New Testaments. If the Bible record is any indication, then winners fast and loser don't."[2]

This is very sobering. I want to be a winner, and I believe you do too.

1. Jentezen Franklin, *Fasting* (Lake Mary, FL: Charisma House, 2008) Pg. 10
2. Mahesh Chavda, *The Hidden Power of Prayer and Fasting* (Shippensburg, PA: Destiny Image, 1998) Pg. 50

Chapter Eight Questions

1. How can we know God wants us to fast and bring breakthrough in our relationships?

2. Describe how breakthroughs can be doors of opportunity.

3. Comment on the statement, "If the Bible record is any indication, then winners fast and loser don't."

4. In what areas do you need significant spiritual breakthroughs in your life?

CHAPTER NINE

Fasting for Financial Breakthrough

> *When you need faith to trust God for big things, fasting is a great way to develop it. Perhaps our biggest challenge to financial breakthrough is not getting money but getting faith...if you are up against a money problem, maybe that is what you need to do—ask for faith.*[1] *— Elmer Towns*

In 2004 my wife and I had been casually looking for a larger house for our growing family. While Janet was on a twenty-one-day fast she coincidently met a lady she had never known before at the hairdressers. She and her husband were selling a home privately at what appeared to be a below-market price. It turned out that the home was an excellent fit for our family. And besides that, they were actually selling two lots in one package: one with the house on it and one vacant lot that could be used for building. It is very unusual for two lots such as those not to be sold separately. We sensed it was the Lord's direction for us to move and we signed for the purchase.

Two months later we needed to sell our current house which was already listed. This time I was on a twenty-one-day fast and my wife and I felt it would sell shortly. On day six of the fast, we had a showing of the house where the public could come through it. At one point there were two parties, one upstairs and one downstairs, bidding against each other, which drove the price up. That day our house sold above our asking price.

Did you follow the significance of that? God opened the door for the new house with a price significantly below market value while my wife was fasting, and we sold our old house above market value while I was fasting. We later built a new house on the separate lot and rented out the original house we bought. Fasting brings financial breakthrough.

As I have already stated, it is hard to imagine what my life would be like without the breakthroughs I have received while fasting. This is true of financial breakthroughs as well. In Elmer Towns' book, *Fasting for Financial Breakthrough*, he teaches that prayer and fasting is the key to putting the role of money in a proper perspective and taking control of our financial future. When fasting I generally keep a journal of what is happening and what God is showing me. My notes written during fasting are peppered with financial breakthroughs.

Many times we find that significant spiritual breakthroughs come with financial breakthroughs as well. This was the experience of Nehemiah. After days of prayer and fasting he received both permission and funding to go build the wall around Jerusalem. How is that for a turn of events?

"Crack the code" fast

As I have fasted and prayed for financial breakthroughs many times the answer comes while on a fast. In 2014, I was praying for funding for a certain ministry for which I am responsible. The funding had reached a certain level and was not going any higher. In one of our meetings an outside consultant stated that we needed to "crack the code." The term "crack the code" refers to breaking a secret spy code or in this context, a barrier that was keeping us from understanding and receiving the information we needed to get the funding to increase. On the first day of the fast this ministry received the single, largest one-time gift it had ever received. This was the financial breakthrough. Why on the first day? I am not sure. As I have stated, it is quite common for something significant to happen on my first day of a fast. Maybe the Lord does this to motivate me to persevere.

The same thing happened to us when looking for investments. In 2008 we were looking around to buy some rental units as an investment and nothing was coming together. However, while on an extended fast, a family member called and said they would sell us the apartment building they owned. Ironically, they had previously turned us down when we requested to buy this property. They also volunteered to sell it to us with no money down and to leave the money in it. That means they did a private mortgage so we didn't even have to go to the bank for financing. Was it just coincidence that this call came while I was fasting? I don't think so.

"Clear the fog" fast

In early 2015 we were experiencing confusion and lack of clarity in a number of areas. One was a rental property we owned that was not performing. Renters were not paying and the property was getting damaged. I was also considering a number of possibilities for overseas trips and just wasn't sure which ones to book. In the midst of this I felt the Lord tell me to go on a "clear the fog" fast to see through all the confusion. Just a couple of days into the fast we received an unexpected, large check from the company we had hired to manage the rental property. They also told us the property had turned around and we would be getting income from it each month going forward. Financial breakthrough. I also was soon able to see which trips to go on and the best times to schedule them. The fog cleared!

Additionally, in 2004 we were considering buying shares in a company. It was the biggest thing we would have done up to that point in the area of business and we would need to borrow the money to do it. It was a unique situation because the company was being transitioned from a non-profit to a for profit company.

We had to have confidence to make this kind of investment. It was on an extended fast that I received the go-ahead. Although it wasn't the best investment we have ever made, it did pay dividends and turned out well for us when we sold it. Probably more important for me was that as one of the owners, I had a seat on the board which gave me a unique education on how to run this kind of a business. What I learned helped change my thinking toward a more prosperous mentality.

Fasting changes your financial thinking

I have spent a lot of my life breaking out of a poverty mindset. Most of the breakthroughs were more about changing my way of thinking about finances than about getting a certain amount of money. A lot of these new ways of thinking came while I was fasting. Listen to Elmer Towns, "We don't get our prayers answered just because we quit eating and start asking. To change the way some of us think and act about money can be a greater miracle than a supernatural supply of money. A transformed attitude about money will glorify God more than winning the lottery."[2] He is correct. As I have prayed and fasted I have found God wants to change my thinking about finances. Occasionally this was opening a new way of thinking more prosperously, but other times it was changing attitudes of my heart.

Because I am responsible for speakers coming to the training school I oversee, I also pay them for teaching. I was sometimes lazy about getting these checks in the mail. When on a fast, the Lord convicted me that not paying these speakers promptly was a form of poor financial stewardship. So I made the change.

I mentioned previously, as the owner of residential rental units, I realized I had become cynical and pronounced judgments on renters who were not paying rent. I realized that my attitude was as bad or worse than their lack of financial integrity. I repented of my judgments. As I changed, the Lord gave me a greater audience of people I could help to get out of poverty and lack.

When God wanted to root poverty thinking out of my own mind, it often happened when I was fasting. One time we were building a fence in our backyard and we did not have enough money to build it with the material that would look the best and last the longest. I was ready to order the lesser quality material, when I felt the Lord say "no." I needed to build it with the better quality fencing. I made the decision and sure enough the money followed. I realized this fence would be something I would see every day in our back yard, and I would be reminded of the Lord's provision every time I saw it.

Many years ago, I was prompted by the Lord to believe for more than "just enough" to get by so that I would have money left over to help others. It was a new concept for me and I was asking the Lord if He really wanted me to do this. It was on a fast that the Lord confirmed this to me and really brought it home to my heart. I was speaking at a church on a Sunday morning about finances and a local man with a prophetic gift spoke to me afterword with the scripture of Jeremiah 1:12: "The LORD said to me, 'You have seen correctly, for I am watching to see that my word is fulfilled.'"

With that confirmation, I left the next day on a trip for some meetings in Europe. My schedule had a long layover in

London, so the person at the flight check-in counter casually asked me if it would be okay to bump me up to first class for the first flight. Of course, I agreed. Since I was in first class I also could use the first class lounge for the London layover. The funny thing was that since I was fasting I couldn't eat any of the really fancy meals on the flight or in the lounge. God's sense of humor I guess…but this event did drive the truth deep in my heart that God wanted to be the God of "more than enough".

On a fast in 1997 I was doing research related to retirement planning and saving. I remember clearly I was in my office praying and I was on the phone on hold with someone to answer some questions about my retirement fund. I saw a funnel. It was gathering money from the whole realm of stocks and securities that were funneled through me and I was redirecting them to places to be used for advancing God's kingdom. I saw that the money would come under my influence and then be channeled where God wants it to be used. It is a picture that has stayed with me until today.

Fasting releases faith for finances

As quoted from Elmer Towns at the beginning of this chapter, our biggest challenge to financial breakthrough is not getting money but getting faith. I hope that all these examples of financial breakthrough as a result of fasting stirs faith in your heart for the same.

1.- Elmer L Towns, *Fasting for Financial Breakthrough* (Ventura, CA: Regal, 2002) Pg. 35
2.- Ibid Pg. 25

Chapter Nine Questions

1. Many times we find significant spiritual breakthrough comes with financial breakthrough. After days of prayer and fasting, Nehemiah received permission to go and build the wall around Jerusalem as well as funding to construct it. Give an example of when you had a spiritual breakthrough that came along with a financial one.

2. How can fasting change your financial thinking?

3. In what area do you need your financial thinking changed?

4. Explain Elmer Towns' quote at the beginning of this chapter, "Our biggest challenge to financial breakthrough is not getting money but getting faith."

CHAPTER TEN

Fasting Will
Birth New Things

> *"Fasting is what prepares you for a new anointing"*[1]
> — Jentezen Franklin

As the father of five children I have observed the birthing process. When a new baby is coming it is exiting, exhilarating, scary and dramatically emotional all at the same time. And that is just from a man's perspective. I can only imagine what it is like from a woman's perspective. It is a traumatic event for the woman's body when a baby is born, but one that is considered by most women to be one of life's most fullfilling experiences. The birth of a baby changes the lives of the parents forever.

Many times a fast can be used by the Lord to birth new things in the life of the one fasting. I have noticed this direct correlation both in the Scriptures and in my life. When a believer shows hunger for God and seeks Him in fasting and prayer, it demonstrates the desire for more. God often responds to this invitation with new visions, new callings, new relationships, new opportunities, new open doors and sometimes new open heavens.

On a recent eight-day fast, the Lord birthed something new in my life. I became increasingly aware of angelic activity around me. I was praying in the woods at a place known for prayer and supernatural visitation when two women approached me asking for directions. One of the women was dressed in all white. We had a casual conversation and eventually the one in white mentioned something about a specific area of gifting that I should be interested in. It occurred to me that she might be an angel, but I didn't think it would be appropriate to say anything then. Later as I reflected on what she had said and the experience, I became more convinced she was an angel that I was entertaining "unaware" (Hebrews 13:2). The gifting, which I first heard from her, was confirmed two additional times within a week.

So much for my experience; let's look at the Scriptures.

Bible examples of fasting starting new things

Luke 2 tells us about an eighty-four-year-old prophetess named Anna. We learn that Anna was devoted to God and that fasting was one expression of her love for Him (verse 37). Anna arrives at the purification of Mary, Joseph and Jesus in the temple forty days after Jesus' birth, as was the custom. The law required that a lamb, two pigeons or two doves be sacrificed after a son's birth.

However, Anna knew the purification of this particular boy was unlike any other. "Coming up to them at that moment, she gave thanks to God and spoke about the child to all who were looking forward to the redemption of Jerusalem" (Luke 2: 38). Anna saw salvation come to Israel in the birth of Jesus. She was an intercessor who spent her time in the temple worshiping, praying and fasting. Through prayer and fasting Anna received insight into things that were hidden from others, and was given the privilege of helping to announce the birth of Jesus and the salvation of Israel.

The forty-day fast of Jesus

Jesus was filled with the Holy Spirit after His baptism and then went on a forty-day fast. Jesus' first miracle of turning water into wine at a wedding in Cana took place at the end of the fast. "What Jesus did here in Cana of Galilee was the first of the signs through which he revealed his glory; and his disciples believed in him" (John 2:11). It is hard to ignore the fact that Jesus' public supernatural ministry was started after an extended fast and the overcoming of Satan's temptation.

As we have noted, the forty-day fast is often related to significant changes in ministry, business or life. Jesus received the Holy Spirit, then fasted for forty days, then performed His first miracle. He received the promise at His baptism. He then fasted, after which the power was released.

History tells us that at the time Jesus was on earth, the Jews observed twenty-two different fast days. They fasted in memory of the soldiers that were killed by the Assyrians four hundred years earlier. They fasted when the Assyrians destroyed several of their cities. Those days of fasting, one after another, were in memory of the losses, the deaths, and the tragic times. In memory of those fallen comrades, they fasted. However, when Jesus fasted forty days, He didn't fast in memory of some depressing thing that happened years earlier. He fasted for something positive. Something new. He fasted so that God would speak to Him, give Him direction and use Him to birth the kingdom of God on earth.

A new measure of faith

Peter, James and John have just come down from the mountain of transfiguration with Jesus. Nine disciples are trying to cast a demon out of a boy—but without success. The boy's father says to Jesus, "These disciples of yours couldn't cast a demon out of my son. Can you help me?" Jesus casts the demon out.

These nine disciples probably already felt badly because they had not been invited to go up the mountain with Jesus when the transfiguration took place. Then they couldn't cast out this demon, perhaps because they were overwhelmed by the outward manifestation of this demon in the boy: throwing him to the ground, making him foam at the mouth and gnash his teeth. Then Jesus was forthright with them and told them they had little faith. Jesus was wondering when they were going to "get it." Ouch. Let's read it:

And He said to them, "Because of the littleness of your faith; for truly I say to you, if you have faith the size of a mustard seed, you will say to this mountain, 'Move from here to there,' and it will move; and nothing will be impossible to you. But this kind does not go out except by prayer and fasting" (Matthew 17:20-21 NASB).

The context here seems to be a teaching on faith. The emphasis of Jesus' response was on faith and not on prayer and fasting. The sole purpose of the praying and fasting in this context was to help their faith, not to cast out devils. We don't need to pray and fast to cast out any devil.

Instead, Jesus was pointing out their unbelief in God's ability. The disciples doubted they could cast out the devil, so He told them about praying and fasting in order to stir up their faith. When you pray and fast, faith is stirred up in you. A new level of faith can be birthed by prayer and fasting. My experience is that when a new level of faith is birthed, it remains permanently at that amplified level in my life and ministry.

More Bible examples

In these examples and throughout the Bible, we see a pattern of fasting connected with birthing new things.

In Genesis 24:33 we see Abraham's servant fasting as he is seeking a bride for Isaac. This was a huge responsibility and he certainly did not want to get it wrong. He responded by fasting. Isaac's wife would carry the seed to birth the Jewish nation.

Moses fasted for forty days when he received the Ten Commandments. God wanted to establish a foundation for His children to live a moral life and He gave this new revelation to a man who was fasting. The Ten Commandments, as we know them today, have become the basis for what most consider a civil society. It is wrong to murder. It is wrong to steal. It is wrong to lie. The lawful protection of what is right and the prevention of wrong are the products of fasting and prayer. This forty-day fast of Moses, where God downloaded His moral code, marked a great achievement for the welfare of all mankind since that time.

In I Samuel we see Hannah (much like Anna) praying and fasting in the temple. Her prayer was for a natural child. After the priest granted her request, she went and got something to eat, ending her fast with the answer to prayer. The child she birthed was Samuel.

Return of the Jews from exile

All three Bible figures that were involved in the return of the Jews from exile fasted and prayed. First there was Daniel who was reading the book of Jeremiah and the Lord highlighted to him that the seventy years of exile would soon be finished. What was his response? He fasted and prayed for the Jews to return from exile. Let's read it:

In the first year of Darius son of Xerxes (a Mede by descent), who was made ruler over the Babylonian kingdom—in the first year of his reign, I, Daniel, understood from the Scriptures, according to the word of the Lord given to Jeremiah the prophet, that the desolation of Jerusalem would last seventy years. So I turned to the Lord God and pleaded with him in prayer and petition, in fasting, and in sackcloth and ashes (Daniel 9:1-3).

Daniel's timely prayer, fasting and intercession worked. The Lord raised up Ezra who would actually return to rebuild the temple. As Ezra was preparing his group to go to build the temple, we find him seeking the Lord in prayer and fasting (Ezra 8:21-23). Ezra didn't want to ask the King for protection so they fasted and prayed and asked the Lord for protection.

Finally we see in Nehemiah 1:4 that Nehemiah was praying and fasting for the restoration of Israel. His part was to rebuild the wall so the exiles could live there safely. His prayer and fasting prepared the way for his audience with the king. King Artaxerxes not only agreed to send Nehemiah to rebuild the wall but also financed his trip. Nehemiah was courageous enough to ask the king for help and it was gladly given to him.

How about writing Scripture?

We see in the Scriptures that David must have done an extended fast to lose as much weight as is described in Psalm 109:24, "My knees give way from fasting; my body is thin and gaunt." David was not interested in what people thought of his appearance. He fasted in mourning and humility; he was only interested in how he could please God. What did David birth? Well…he was a writer who wrote much of the book of Psalms. Also Paul, a man given to prayer and fasting, wrote a lot of the New Testament.

Fasting at Azusa Street

When God desired to breathe a Holy Spirit movement on the earth in the 20th Century, He did so through a gathering of fasting believers in Los Angles, California. The Azusa street revival in 1906 started with ten days of fasting and prayer. A few people came to Los Angles and fasted and prayed for ten days and the Holy Spirit fell upon the place. William Seymore was the humble leader of this great spiritual outpouring. An eyewitness said, "I had the room adjoining brother Seymore. I know that brother Seymore, who was the leader of the Azusa folk, fasted for weeks at a time and only ate occasionally. There was much fasting and prayer in those days…" Another eyewitness said, "The first thing that was done before the power ever fell on Azusa was a united ten-day season of fasting and prayer."[1]

What many church historians now call the "Second Pentecost" is credited with birthing the many Pentecostal denominations that number over seven hundred today. Currently, there are more than 280 million Pentecostals worldwide and the movement is growing in many parts of the world, especially the global south. All of these denominations can trace their roots back to the Azusa Street revival. Many other Protestant, Catholic and missions movements have also embraced the Pentecostal experience.

Many believe the early disciples were fasting in the upper room preparing the way for the first Pentecost. Indeed it is hard to imagine that they would be sitting down to eat full meals as they were praying and waiting in this faith-charged atmosphere of the upper room.

Fasting for church planting

Our pastor friend Yona and his wife were planting a new church in the state of Haryana in India. They were attempting to evangelize without any success in this strongly Hindu area. Yona decided to go on a twenty-one-day fast. The day after he finished the fast, he went to pray for a Hindu man with tuberculosis that the doctors had given no hope for recovery. The man was healed, and he and eventually his family became Christians.

On the second day after the fast was finished he went to pray for an eighteen-year-old lady who could not speak. Again the hospital had no remedy for her and it appeared that demons were keeping her from speaking. Yona prayed for her and asked her to say "Hallelujah." There was no response. He asked again…and again. The third time he asked her to speak she was able to say "Hallelujah." She was delivered and healed—and also came to Christ. The church was planted.

Subsequently over four hundred new believers were baptized and a number of additional churches were planted.

Conclusion

Time and again we see God initiating or birthing new things through believers who are fasting and praying. What does God want to birth in your life? Are you bored with your Christian life? Does it feel like you are doing the same thing year after year? Are you praying the same prayers year after year with only limited answers?

Franklin Hall would say if you have even one prayer that is not answered you should begin to fast immediately.[2] Fasting is a spiritual exercise that demonstrates to the Lord that you are looking for more, for something new in your life. When the Lord births something new in your life, many times it will ultimately lead to you in turn birthing something new in the world around you.

1.   Jentezen Franklin, *Fasting* (Lake Mary, FL: Charisma House, 2008) Pg. 48
2.   Franklin Hall, *The Fasting Prayer* (San Diego, CA: Self published, 1952) Pg. 27

Chapter Ten Questions

1.   Name some examples in the Bible in which fasting brought the start of something new.

2.   What have you learned about the Azusa Street spiritual awakening?

3. What was Jesus talking about when He said, 'This kind does not come out but by prayer and fasting" (Mark 9:29)?

4. What new thing does God want to birth or establish in your life?

5. What does fasting demonstrate to the Lord?

CHAPTER ELEVEN

Don't Separate Fasting from the Written Word

> *Fasting is a grace that significantly increases our receptivity to the Lord's voice and His Word. It allows us to enter into depths in our relationship with God that are beyond what we normally experience.*[1]
> — Mike Bickle

A friend of mine who is an itinerant teacher and prophetic minister has told me of at least forty different people who shared with him privately they were fully convinced they were one of the two witnesses spoken of in the book of Revelation. A number of these arrived at this conclusion after times of extended fasting and prayer. This is problematic. First of all, there are only two witnesses spoken of in Revelation, so most of them have to be wrong. Secondly, it is clear that fasting without accountability and grounding in the Bible can lead to deception.

Whenever I am on a fast I try to take extra time reading the Word of God. When fasting, believers should spend time reading the Word and be in prayer, and have others pray for them as well. Fasting is a doorway into the spirit world and the Word of God keeps us from getting weird or being deceived. Certainly fasting is a great opportunity for us to hear God's voice, see breakthrough in our lives and experience His love and presence in dynamic ways. However, there is also the possibility that we could be spiritually deceived. We have none other than Jesus to look to as an example. He used the Word to rebuke Satan at the end of his forty-day fast. The Word of God brought victory.

Sincere believers who go on long fasts must have a strong foundation in the Bible. If not they can be deceived with delusional ideas. Fasting cannot be approached without a commitment to the Word of God and practical accountability. A Christian might fast for forty days and think of him or herself as super spiritual. Pride can enter in and someone can begin to think they don't need a church, parents or a pastor. Not true. Every believer needs accountability and needs to be submitted to a pastor.

We understand from the Scriptures there is a physical world and a spiritual world. Most human beings live their lives in the physical world with only minimal involvement in the spirit world. God created the spirit world. It is real. There are legal (by the Holy Sprit) and illegal (pagan) ways of accessing it. Fasting is a spiritual experience. As the human body is quieted the human spirit soars. It is a spiritual experience which allows us to enter legally (scripturally) into the spirit world. As previously mentioned, Franklin Hall said, "Food abstinence allows man to get closer to the spirit realm than by any other way."[2]

Why is this important? Buddhists fast, too. They enter a spiritual place but do it illegally. They want to become impersonal and enter a spiritual place to escape the natural world and indeed they do have spiritual experiences. Instead of this unbiblical approach, the Christian is invited by the Holy Spirit to blend our person with God's person, our spirit with the Holy Spirit. The Scriptures call this the fellowship of the Holy Spirit (2 Corinthians 3:14).

I know that every revelation and experience I receive while fasting must be compared to the Scriptures for affirmation. If it is not scriptural I throw it out. If it is not clear...I put it on the shelf and wait for other confirmation. Even though I have thirty-five years of walking with the Lord and ministry experience, I know I can be deceived and need accountability in my life. Mike Bickle says it this way:

> Fasting sensitizes the human spirit to the spirit realm, including both the Godly and the occult realms. Many false religions and occult groups encourage fasting because they know it releases power. They are often led by people committed to fasting who deny their flesh to have greater access to the spirit realm. Many of the major false religions on the earth were started by those who were engaged in extreme seasons of prayer and fasting...The eastern religions practice fasting that is preoccupied with self, as their followers seek to earn

God's blessing. But the Scriptures teach us to fast to strengthen us in our quest to be preoccupied with God and his will.[3]

The believer who is fasting must be in submission to what I call the Lordship of God's written Word. It is the standard by which every revelation is measured. Most heresy throughout church history has come as a result of people acting in the flesh and doing things that are not fully explained in the Word.

The Spirit and the Word

The Spirit and the Word always agree (1 John 5:7, 8). The Spirit inspired the Word and will never contradict it. No one can claim illumination of the Spirit if that 'illumination' conflicts with the written Word of God. The Spirit will never communicate a revelation which is in contradiction with Scripture itself. Simply stated, we already know the Holy Spirit wrote the Bible so He will not speak anything to us that contradicts the Bible or He would be disagreeing with Himself. When we get revelation or insight that is not clearly affirmed or prohibited in the Bible, we need the accountability of spiritual authorities and a church community to help with discernment.

Both Peter and Paul based their message and ministry on the Scriptures and used them as a basis to build on in hearing God's voice. Rick Joyner in his book *A Prophetic Vision for the 21st Century* speaks to this same idea:

The apostle Paul's knowledge of the Scriptures gave him a profound understanding of Christ and the new covenant, as well as God's general plan to extend His ministry of reconciliation and His plan for Paul to go to the gentiles with that ministry. However when the Lord wanted Paul to go to Macedonia, Scripture could not give him that direction; he had to know the voice of the Lord (Acts 16:9-10). We see the same pattern in Peter's life…when the Lord needed to give him special guidance, such as the commission to go to Cornelius's house to be the first to preach the gospel to the Gentiles, the Lord gave him a special vision Acts (10:9-48). Peter first obeyed the leading of the Holy Spirit, and then went to Jerusalem to confirm what he had done with the elders. Finally they all turned to the Scriptures.[3]

As we are fasting we must honor all three things we are discussing: hearing God's voice, the Lordship of the Scriptures and accountability in a relational community. As a three-legged stool forms a level seat to sit on, these three form a level foundation for believers to fast. With this caution in place I want to be clear that fasting prepares the way for God to communicate clearly with you, to give you fresh revelations, and clear purpose.

Lag

Occasionally the opposite happens. Instead of great spiritual revelation, experiences with God and prophetic insights, it doesn't seem like anything is happening while we are fasting. We might even feel spiritually dry. Again, fasting cannot be separated from the Word of God. The Word says fasting works and so we believe it does and expect results even though we don't see them. Sometimes fasting is misunderstood because many times people can't see or feel what fasting is doing while it is in progress. Franklin Hall says, "The spiritual success of fasting cannot always be measured while fasting, but many victories are gained later. Folks cannot always see or feel what fasting is doing while it is in progress. It produces because Jesus said it would."[5]

Delayed gratification

Fasting is delayed gratification. It involves giving up a current pleasure (food) for future greater reward. To explain this concept, we will look at an example from American football.

One of the most watched television events in the world is the Super Bowl. Over 100 million people watch the telecast of the Super Bowl, the championship game for American football. A team that appears in the Super Bowl game on a regular basis is the New England Patriots. Since the early 2000s the Patriots have been to the playoffs fifteen times, won nine conference championships and five Super Bowls. So whether you like the Patriots or not you still have to be impressed with their success and observe what can be learned from it.

How can the Patriots be so good for so long? One answer is delayed gratification.

The Patriots learned years ago that other NFL teams display a high degree of impatience. They found that almost all NFL teams overconfidently believed they had a realistic chance to build a Super Bowl team immediately, to the point that during the draft of new players from college teams, they anxiously trade to get higher round picks for a certain player they think will make their team immediately better. To do this they agree to give up high draft picks in future years.

I will give a specific illustration. In 2012 the Washington Redskins desperately wanted a college quarterback from Baylor University, Robert Griffin III. They acquired the number two overall pick in the draft to get Mr. Griffin by giving another team four very high-value draft picks over three years—first-round picks in 2012, 2013 and 2014 and a second-round pick in 2012. Mr. Griffin played only three seasons for the Redskins before suffering a series of injuries; he is no longer with the Redskins. The trade left the Redskins in a hole for many years, without draft picks to sign new talent. Can you picture Esau trading his birthright for a hot bowl of soup when he was hungry?

A smart NFL front office could exploit the other teams' impatience by systematically trading their current year's picks for higher-value ones in future years. The Patriots head coach Bill Belichick used this insight in seven of the eighteen NFL drafts during his tenure with great success. He was willing to give up one player for numerous players in the years to come that lifted the whole level of talent on his teams and led to many championships.[6]

I call this delayed gratification. So for someone in Africa this could mean not buying a new suit with the proceeds of the corn harvest and instead buying a cow that will provide income for years. After ten years this person can buy as many new suits as they want. For others in the Western world it might mean not spending all their income and saving ten percent for future investments. Perhaps foregoing the cost of a vacation and investing that amount of money to have the possibility of many vacations in the future or, as Christians, to have the possibility to give away more money in the future.

This is the nature of fasting. It demonstrates to God the will to give up short-term "feel good" moments for long-term success or breakthrough.

Fasting is an amazing discipline. It puts legs to our prayers and adds power to them. I like to think of fasting as a multiplier of our prayers. It will be worth all the waiting and struggling when we see the results.

1. Mike Bickle, *The Rewards of Fasting* (Kansas City, MI: Forerunner, 2005) Pg. 6
2. Franklin Hall, *The Fasting Prayer* (San Diego, CA: Self published, 1952) Pg. 144
3. Ibid Pg. 118, Pg. 6
4. Rick Joyner, *A Prophetic Vision for the 21st Century* (Nashville, TN: Thomas Nelson, 1999) Pg. 83
5. Franklin Hall, *The Fasting Prayer* (San Diego, CA: Self published, 1952) Pg. 144
6. *Behavioral Economics May Make Champs of the Cleveland Browns...* Following the advice of an academic paper, the team improved from 0-16 in 2017 to 7-8-1 last year. By Jon Hartley. Feb. 1, 2019 Wall Street Journal

Chapter Eleven Questions

1. Why should you be sure to do a lot of Bible reading while fasting?

2. Why is practical accountability important while fasting?

3. How do we know the Holy Spirit will never speak anything that disagrees with the written Word of God?

4. What is meant by the term *lag* in relation to fasting?

CHAPTER TWELVE

How Long
Shall I Fast?

> *You don't have to go on dramatically long fasts to get the benefits of fasting...The critical element is not the length of the fast, but that you yield to His leading. If you have never fasted in your life the Lord would be happy to meet you in a one or three-day fast.[1]*
> — *Mahesh Chavda.*

Jesus did it. He fasted. So that provides the example for us. He said that after He left this earth, His disciples would fast. "Jesus answered, 'How can the guests of the bridegroom mourn while he is with them? The time will come when the bridegroom will be taken from them; then they will fast'" (Matthew 9:15). He didn't say His followers *might* fast, but that "they will." We can do it. It is only a question of how often and how long.

Does this sound legalistic? It is not. The length and frequency of your fasting is up to you and the Holy Spirit. Although I am a wholehearted believer in fasting and do so frequently, for two separate years out of the last twenty I did not fast at all...not a single day. This was because I did not have the leading of the Holy Spirit to fast.

In the Bible we see certain numbers that have different meanings associated with them. Some of these numbers are associated with fasting and allow for creativity in fasting as well as us learning to hear His voice. As you might recall I was quite amazed when I read that Mahesh Chavda did two forty-day fasts and two twenty-one-day fasts each year. This is an example of different lengths of fasting. Let's look at different numbers and their meanings as applied to the length of a fast.

One-day fast

The one-day fast carries with it the idea of cleansing, unity with God and the Lordship of Jesus Christ. In Bible times, fasts were often one day in length. Judges 20:26 says, "Then the Israelistes, all the people, went up to Bethel, and there they sat weeping before the Lord. They fasted that day until evening and presented burnt offerings and fellowship offerings to the Lord."

Three-day fast

The three-day fast is associated with establishing a foundation and deliverance, especially for a new Christian. In Acts 9:9 Paul fasted three days after meeting Jesus until the time he met Cornelius and received his sight. When individuals come to me desiring to be free from smoking, pornography or other habits or addictions, I generally encourage them to go on a three-day fast as a path to freedom. The three-day fast can "loose the bonds of wickedness" as stated in Isaiah 58:6.

Larry Kreider gives the following account of a three-day fast in his book *Speak Lord*:

> One of our churches' small groups witnessed first-hand the power of prayer and fasting. A woman in their group could not kick a drug habit. They had been praying for Sarah for quite some time. Finally the small group said, "Lord, we really just want her to follow after you; do whatever it takes Lord!" They initiated a three-day prayer and fast. Many in the group had never been on a fast before, but they fasted and prayed nonetheless. On the third day, Sarah was getting high with a friend, and they started talking about God. As Sarah drove home that day, the Lord spoke clearly to her spirit. She heard him say, "I am the way."
>
> A bit unnerved, Sarah immediately drove to her sister's apartment. She said, "I don't know what just happened exactly, but I think God just spoke to me and said He was 'the way.' What is this? What's it all about?" As they began to talk, Sarah gave her life to Jesus, flushed all her drugs down the drain, got baptized and testified in the small group of the goodness of the Lord.[2]

Because a team of Christians had circled around a broken-hearted sister with a three-day fast, God brought freedom in a powerful way.

The three-day fast can also quickly be enacted during a time of crisis. As mentioned earlier we find Esther fasting when her people were at risk of genocide in Esther 4:15-16. It was a three-day fast.

> Then Esther sent this reply to Mordecai: "Go, gather together all the Jews who are in Susa, and fast for me. Do not eat or drink for three days, night or day. I and my attendants will fast as you do. When this is done, I will go to the king, even though it is against the law. And if I perish, I perish."

Esther called a fast for her people in a time of crisis. They fasted before she went to the king. But in crisis we do not always have this option.

One time a good friend of ours who attended our local church was rushed to the hospital with strange, hard to diagnose medical symptoms. All, including the doctors, were puzzled by the life-threatening situation she was in. In this time of crisis, I felt impressed of the Lord to go on a three-day fast starting immediately. As her condition worsened I continued my fast. On day three, the medical condition was diagnosed accurately, and treatment was found that brought her back to good health. Both my fast and the crisis were over.

Five-day fast

When I consider the number five as it relates to fasting, I notice primarily it is a fast associated with grace. In Ephesians 4:11-12 we find the fivefold ministry given to prepare and perfect the saints for ministry out of God's grace. Some are called to be apostles, prophets, evangelists, pastors or teachers. In addition we see the number five associated with God's grace in the structure of the tabernacle in the wilderness in Exodus 26:26-27. It provided a meeting place for God and His people. The pillars were five cubits apart and five cubits high. The brazen altar was five cubits by five cubits. There were five pillars at the end of the Holy Place. The tabernacle symbolized God's grace later to be revealed in the new covenant.

A five-day fast could as well be a time of preparation for an event or season of your life. The five wise virgins were prepared. David, in preparing for Goliath, took up five smooth stones. We can't forget that Jesus took five loaves to feed five thousand. It led to multiplication and abundance.

Seven-day fast

The seven-day fast has the concept of Sabbath associated with it. This means awakening, refreshment and rest. Of course God rested on the seventh day of creation. For us the principle of Sabbath means to stop, look back, look up to God and look ahead. What a great thing to do on a fast. It was on a seven-day fast that I received a sense of completion and the freedom to resign from a board on which I was serving and to take on a primary leadership role on another board.

I believe a seven-day fast can also have victory and breakthrough associated with it. The number seven is related to the fall of Jericho in the Joshua 6:1-20. "And seven priests shall bear seven trumpets of rams' horns before the ark. But the seventh day you shall march around the city seven times, and the priests shall blow the trumpets" (Joshua 6:4, NKJV). The city of Jericho stood between the children of Israel and their inhabition of the Promised Land. God wants his children today to possess their promised lands.

Eight-day fast

When I sense the Lord is asking me to go on an eight-day fast it usually means there are new beginnings in store. In the Bible we find the number eight associated with and symbolizing new beginnings. There were seven days of creation and on the eighth day, life began on the earth.

In the time of Noah the whole world was destroyed, but when Noah's ark rested on Mt. Ararat, eight people emerged to a new beginning of life on earth. Interestingly enough, the writers of the New Testament were eight in number: Matthew, Mark, Luke, John, Paul, James, Peter and Jude. The New Testament was a new beginning in God's relationship with mankind. It was while on an eight-day fast that I received a revelation for a new beginning in our finances. It was the transition from being debt based to asset based.

Twelve-day fast

The twelve-day fast seems to have an association with the increase of authority, responsibility or leadership. In the Bible the number twelve signifies government, order or rule.

For example it was the twelve tribes of Israel that spoke to organization and to leadership of Israel. The dimensions of the heavenly city of New Jerusalem have multiples of the number twelve. Jesus had twelve apostles on which the church was built. The apostolic ministry might be associated with this fast: an increase of authority, especially spiritual authority.

I noticed a significant increase of leadership favor in our community during one twelve-day fast. I was given wisdom and confidence to handle very difficult, complex, relational challenges with some individuals in our community. I had wisdom to respond to each person and situation during what many considered to be a community crisis. I emerged with respect from all parties.

Twenty-one-day fast

I believe the twenty-one-day fast is associated with revelation and hearing God's voice. We already talked about the story of Daniel when he fasted for twenty-one days and an angel appeared to him and said, "Since the first day that you set your mind to gain understanding...I have come in response....I have come to explain to you what will happen" (Daniel 10:12-14). Daniel was asking the Lord a question, and the answer came as he was fasting.

We read that Daniel was overcome by the supernatural presence of God's messenger on this twenty-one-day fast. Without going into detail, I must honestly say that I have experienced similar situations while on a twenty-one-day fast.

As I look at the notes I have taken during my twenty-one-day fasts I notice that I have received numerous significant revelations during these fasts. Some revelations relate to the nature and character of God, but others relate to actions I need and want to take. With the revelation of actions to take also came the boldness and confidence to take them because I knew they were from God. In one particularly challenging situation, I received clear understanding of what the Lord was doing behind the scenes. This gave me confidence to persevere.

Forty-day fast

To me, the forty-day fast has the deepest amount of humility associated with it. It includes testing because of its length and also an enjoyable brokenness. One clear pattern we see with the forty-day fast is transition in ministry. Why? Because as we observed, it was after the forty-day fast that Jesus started His ministry and did His first miracle as recorded in Matthew 4:1-2 and John 2:9, 11: "Then Jesus was led by the Spirit into the wilderness to be tempted by the devil. After fasting forty days and forty nights, he was hungry."... "And the master of the banquet tasted the water that had been turned into wine... This, the first of his miraculous signs, Jesus performed at Cana in Galilee. He thus revealed his glory, and his disciples put their faith in him."

I have noticed that often following a forty-day fast, new opportunities are open. Franklin Hall said this; "Any adult can fast forty days, feel young and have tremendous power with

God. In twenty days, cleansing has occurred. Focus on Jesus and a dramatic focus will be reached. Thirty-five to forty-five days is like drilling for oil, a certain depth is reached little by little—a gusher-intimate closeness to Jesus. Your capacity will be enlarged."[3] This is a compelling invitation to experience more of Jesus and possibly transition in your life or ministry.

Three highly developed spiritual leaders of the Bible, Jesus, Moses and Elijah, fasted for the full length of forty days. Moses fasted forty days on Mount Sinai receiving God's Law and another forty days on the mountain after the golden calf sin. Elijah, some three hundred years later, spent forty days on the same mountain worshiping God. When the apostle James wanted to select a man who was an example of "effectual fervent prayer," he chose Elijah, a man who went for forty days without eating. Franklin Hall said this about the forty-day fast. "So why is forty days so significant? It is a time of testing and preparation for things ahead. It will also develop a greater amount of the fruit, humility and patience that will be needed."[4]

Holiness and humility are the main themes of this fast. One time while on a forty-day fast God told me, "What is it to you if I work on your character for forty years, before I give you thirty years of power?" My conclusion was, "Sure. You are God and I am not."

The length of the fasts mentioned in this chapter are significant, however they are not the only way God has led me in fasting. Sometimes these numbers are combined. Sometimes

God gives me a theme for a fast that is more important than the length. We will examine theme fasts in the next chapter.

1. Mahesh *Chavda, The Hidden Power of Prayer and Fasting* (Shippensburg, PA: Destiny Image, 1998) pg. 34
2. Larry Kreider, *Speak Lord I'm Listening* (Ventura, CA: Regal, 2008) Pg. 37
3. Franklin Hall, *The Fasting Prayer* (San Diego, CA: Self published, 1952) Pg. 154
4. Ibid, Pg. 158

Chapter Twelve Questions

1. What is the longest you have ever fasted? How will you know if God wants you to fast longer than this?

2. What people would you ask to pray for you while you are fasting?

3. What length of fast appeals to you as a good challenge?

4. Would you ever consider at forty-day fast? Why or why not?

CHAPTER THIRTEEN

Theme
Fasts

> *I finished fasting yesterday, and it was an incredible experience! The encounters I had with the Lord were so intimate. There was so much deposited into me regarding the specific things I was seeking God for— far more than I could have asked or even imagined. My life has truly been marked by God in a deeper way during this fast.* — Matt

Sometimes the Lord will give me a theme for a particular fast that helps direct its outcome or content. I already mentioned my "Crack the code" and "Clear the fog" fast. Theme fasts have been some of my most amazing. Sometimes you don't know the theme until during the fast or even after it is over. Then something God spoke to you becomes so significant in your life that you remember the fast by that revelation.

The wedding fast

A few years ago, I felt the Lord wanted me to fast for twenty-one days, but could not find a time in my schedule to do it. It was summer and I was looking at my calendar and talking to my wife about a time to fit it in. I have learned to always bring my wife in on the decision of when I will fast so that we can be in agreement. I totally understand that she does not want me to be "Mr. Spiritual" and be fasting during a big family gathering picnic or meal, so we try to plan around those things. Who wants to be fasting on Thanksgiving or Christmas? Don't do it! Enjoy these times and celebrate God's goodness with family and friends.

So, I couldn't quite fit in the twenty-one days but then noticed that we had two weddings about three weeks apart. I excitedly counted up the days, but to my dismay found it was actually twenty days between the weddings and not twenty-one. I was disappointed. But my wife said, "Get over it. Just fast between the two weddings." So I did.

It was amazing. The weddings were twenty days apart. At the second wedding I was overwhelmed as God showed me the love He has for His bride, the church. I cried when I realized how He looks on His church with such passion and lavish love. During the song *How Beautiful is the Body of Christ* there was a professional dancer doing a prophetic dance. During the dance, a little flower girl fell asleep right on the stage and the dancer was lovingly dancing around her as she slept. It was such a beautiful picture communicating His love and protection for us. It was powerful. I experienced a deep revelation of God's love.

Jubilee fast

When I turned age fifty I felt the Lord directing me to go on a twenty-one-day fast. This became my Jubilee fast. The number fifty in the Bible is associated with the Year of Jubilee. It means a refresh, a reset or a new start. In the year of Jubilee in Israel all the land that was lost, sold or earned was returned to the original owners. Debts were canceled and obligations forgiven. It was like a fresh start that takes place once in a lifetime. God's favor and approval are part of the Year of Jubilee.

During this Jubilee fast the Lord showed me I should forgive myself for the mistakes I made in my first fifty years. So I wrote down what I considered to be the seven biggest mistakes I made in leadership and ministry and went through each one and forgave myself for those mistakes. Wow! What freedom I experienced. In one case I actually had a clothing article that had the logo and name of one of my greatest failures printed on it. When I forgave myself for that mistake I literally walked out of the building I was in and threw the shirt into a trash container outside. It was over and behind; I could move on to the new things God had for me.

Sabbath fast

One year I felt the Lord leading me to go on a twenty-one-day fast in January to start the year. As I looked at my schedule and counted days I just couldn't find three consecutive weeks that didn't conflict with a family or social outing that was important to me and my wife. I kept praying and looking for a way to do it. Finally I spotted three seven-day segments of the month that were open. Oh...three sevens is twenty-one days. Since a seven-day fast is generally a Sabbath fast and Sabbath means looking back, looking up and looking ahead then I could take the first week to look back at the successes and failures of the previous year, the second week of fasting to look up and connect with God again in prayer and the last week would to pray for vision and direction for the year ahead. This Sabbath fast got me off to a great start for the year. It totaled twenty-one days but was not twenty-one continuous days. I love this creative leading of the Holy Spirit in fasting.

"I want it all" fast

In 2015 while I was on a fast the Lord was showing me the following year was going to be a year of opportunity. He gave me the name *I Want It All* for this fast. Interestingly enough, I realized I was experiencing what is called opportunity loss with a business endeavor of which we were part owners. Opportunity loss means you are missing an unknown future opportunity because energy and focus is going in to maintaining something that is not really going anywhere. We started to take steps to sell this business so we would be ready for the new opportunity.

It seemed like everything God showed me on this fast lined up with the "I want it all" theme. I received direction from the Lord to go on a forty-day fast in the upcoming year. I also was able to settle on the culminating project for my masters program and the one I chose became an initiative that is a growing blessing to people today.

Corporate fasts

A specific type of theme fast is when a church or a group of individuals fast together. The Bible calls this a sacred assembly. Joel 1:14 states "Declare a holy fast; call a sacred assembly. Summon the elders and all who live in the land to the house of the Lord your God, and cry out to the Lord." Corporate fasting adds accountability and strength to our prayers.

Here is the testimony of one church seeking the Lord with a corporate fast as told by the church's Senior Pastor, Deryl Hurst.

Near the end of 2012 I felt like our church needed to experience revival and renewal. I had been doing some reading on the spiritual discipline of fasting and felt like God was calling the church to begin 2013 by giving "the first fruits" unto God, much like tithing. I felt God was calling our church to begin 2013 with a twenty-one-day fast. I knew that as the leader of the church, I would need to set the example and lead the way.

Ultimately I made the commitment to fast the entire twenty-one days taking in water and juice, but no food at all. I challenged the church that I felt like each person should engage at some level. It could be a Daniel fast, perhaps just one day in each of the three weeks, or maybe fast one meal each day for the twenty-one days. Others, I felt, would be called to join me in fasting the entire twenty-one days. But I challenged each of them to hear God and be obedient to what He was calling them to do. I ended 2012 with a message on why we fast and what the Bible has to say about it.

Our people did engage and nearly everyone committed to fast in some way. The twenty-one days were difficult physically for me and good spiritually. However nothing particularly earth shattering happened during that fast and I ended it mildly disappointed, yet full of faith that we had been obedient, and confident that God would do His part and honor His word.

Then came the "suddenly." On Sunday morning February 3, 2013, about ten days after our fast ended, I was in our auditorium as usual prior to the service, praying for the service as the worship team was doing their normal rehearsal.

Suddenly in that empty room with just the worship team, the sound guy, and me, the powerful presence of the Holy Spirit fell in a way that I can't begin to describe. I was so overcome that I began to weep and sob, basking in His presence. I had to preach later and knew I had to regain my composure. I headed over to our conference room for our pre-service prayer with our pastors, elders, and other leaders, thinking that would help. It was to no avail. I am reminded of the words of Isaiah when he came into the presence of God "Woe is me, I am undone, I am a man of unclean lips and live among a people of unclean lips." I was undone, and wept the entire prayer time.

The people walking into the auditorium that morning had no idea what they were walking into. As soon as our worship started, the Presence enveloped the room and nearly everyone was undone. There was weeping, praising, prophetic words, but most of all, there was the Presence of the Almighty God. It was healing, transforming, convicting, refreshing—it was wonderful. This powerful presence of the Holy Spirit continued for many weeks bringing with it the revival and renewal we needed.

God is true to His word; when we do our part in obedience, He will do His part!

Corporate fasts during crisis or leadership change

Jehoshaphat called a corporate fast in a time of crisis when the armies of Moab and Ammon confronted him. God gave them the victory. We have already discussed how Esther asked all the people of Israel to fast with her when they were facing destruction. The early church fasted and prayed their way through another time of crisis when Peter was in prison. The results speak for themselves.

Local churches considering major financial decisions or leadership decisions might want to call a corporate fast. In Acts 14:23 the early church did just that: "Paul and Barnabas appointed elders for them in each church and, with prayer and fasting, committed them to the Lord, in whom they had put their trust." This is a good example for us today.

The Daniel fast

A great way for a church or group to do a corporate fast is called the Daniel fast. It is generally considered to be eating only fruits, vegetables, nuts and juices for a certain amount of time, abstaining from meats, alcohol and rich foods. Some people use the Daniel fast instead of fasting from food entirely. This gives people flexibility during a corporate fast.

Daniel knew the power of prayer and fasting. He and his three friends chose to eat only these foods and the results were amazing. There is more specific information about the Daniel fast found in Appendix B. It is good to be aware that the Lord might give spiritual insight during a Daniel fast as stated in Daniel 1:17, "...to these four young men God gave knowledge and understanding."

Husbands and wives fasting together

Many times husbands and wives find a greater oneness and unity by fasting together. On one of my forty-day fasts my wife decided to join me for the second half of the fast. At this time she had not fasted for many years so, to be honest, I was a little skeptical. But I took her at her word and she did it. I was quite impressed with her resolve, and it did lead to a greater oneness in our relationship.

In the next chapter we will look at some practical tips and mistakes to avoid.

Chapter Thirteen Questions

1. What is meant by a "theme fast"?

2. Describe a corporate fast you have been on.

3. What is a Daniel fast and why is it effective?

4. Why can it create a greater oneness in their marriage when husbands and wives fast together?

CHAPTER FOURTEEN

Practical Tips
and Mistakes to Avoid

> *Fasting is not scary...it is the Christian lifestyle. This should be a practical life discipline of every believer. It is not as hard as we think it is. It is attainable for the ordinary, average, weak, pizza-loving, twenty-some-thing person...you will see it make a huge difference in your life.[1]* — Dwayne Roberts

I am a very practical person. I cannot give you all this teaching, encouragement to fast and stories of breakthroughs while fasting, without giving you the practical tools to do it successfully. Jesus led the way with fasting Himself and instructing His disciples to do likewise after He left. As mentioned before, we can be sure Jesus fasted a natural fast on water like we do. In other words, God did not supernaturally sustain Him. When He was tempted in the wilderness He was tempted with food because He was physically hungry. Satan knew He wasn't thirsty, because did not tempt Him with water. He said, "Tell these stones to become bread" (Matthew 4:3).

Paul was quite open to talk about his frequent fasts as an example for others. Both Jesus and Paul knew that fasting would not be easy so they set the example by doing it themselves.

The following are practical insights about fasting. They will help you navigate your way through an extended fast and hopefully see a lot of fruit from it.

Fast specifically

After you have determined how long to fast, ask God for specific focuses or targets for your fast. Dr. Fomum speaks to this idea, "There is room for general fasting, but the great moves in fasting are when people have an overriding request."[2] When I fast I usually ask the Lord for things to pray for on different levels. For example, I might be praying for something specifically for my family or myself, but then also have a focus for our local church or a ministry that I am leading. In addition to this I might have a national focus to pray for or possibly a nation outside of my own. Another level might be a specific person, leader or business for which I am praying. Of course a great focus is just to grow in intimacy with the Lord as well.

I grab a tablet or legal pad and list these things on the first page. Then I start a log of things that happen on each day as I am fasting. If I am feeling weak, I write it down. When I see breakthrough or answers I write those down as well. Many times the Lord highlights scriptures that I write down,. There could be unexpected phone calls that come or other important information; I write all these things. Not every day is dynamic, but it can get very exciting seeing what God is doing and speaking to us. I note when God speaks something to do or for me to learn. On one of my forty-day fasts, I received sixty-four significant takeaways or insights. When the fast is over, I summarize these results and what I have heard from God. I try not to make any major decisions until after the fast is over and I can reflect on what God has been saying.

Fast to control the flesh?

Fasting is not done to control the flesh. (That is a called a diet). Fasting is a spiritual pursuit. However, it does have physical benefits. You will lose weight when fasting, but it is generally gained back with care if the fast is ended properly. Don't go on a fast to lose weight. For the person who is overweight it is better to lose weight by growing in discipline before the fast is started.

Fasting on mostly water

Okay. This is my experience and I will tell you my story. As I mentioned before when I first started to fast I would drink a lot of liquids beside juices, including milkshakes and anything else I could liquefy by putting it in the blender. I eventually cut back to just juices. However when I read some of the fasting experts from church history like Franklin Hall,

I realized they talked about fasting on just water. This got my attention so I started to consider this.

When drinking juice I would have a couple of large glasses of juice at breakfast, then a couple more at lunch, then some more at dinner time, followed by a glass of juice (or two) before bed. The more I considered this, I realized that the juice I had at breakfast time seemed like a meal. It seemed like breakfast. And the juice I was drinking at lunch seemed like I was eating lunch. So was I fasting or just eating juice for a meal? I decided I would experiment with drinking water only while fasting.

So, I would start a twenty-one-day fast and drink juice for seven days, and then switch to water only for the next seven days and finish the last seven days drinking juice again. This worked well for a while but then I noticed when I switched from juice to water it was as physically demanding as when I started the fast. It was like starting the fast all over again. So I decided to try fasting on water only.

A fast with only water was a good experience physically and spiritually. It is just amazing how well you get to know your body and what your body can do. There were a few downsides though. At times I would get too weak and frighten the people around me, or I would not be at full energy for a meeting and feel like this was not respectful for the others attending. Another thing about drinking water for twenty-one or forty days is that you get bored with it. Water can be cold, hot or warm...that is it. So eventually I arrived at what I call a mostly water fast.

The mostly water fast is drinking as much water as possible. I add some lemon or lime juice to give it some flavor or make a cup of decaf tea with a spoon of sugar. When I drink juice, especially if it is an acidy juice like orange juice, I mix water with it at a ratio of half and half. If I need energy for a meeting or a specific physical activity I will drink some juice that allows me to contribute without disappointing others. So I could be drinking some juice each day, mostly diluted. That is what I have done and still do when fasting. Please don't think this is a rule for everyone. I still do the Daniel fast occasionally too. It is better to fast eating and drinking at the level you have faith for than to not fast at all.

If you are working on a job that involves heavy physical labor, drink juice during your fast. Franklin Hall suggested a three-day fast on only water and then five hundred calories a day in juices for the forty-day duration.

How to start a fast

If you have never fasted, start gradually with a shorter fast. Don't start with forty days. Three or seven days are a good warm-up. Just challenge yourself to fast longer or more than you have before possibly up to forty days. Although I know some who have done it, I have never fasted longer than forty days.

Before the start date of your fast begin to prepare yourself physically. Cut back to eating only fruit, vegetables and simple foods in the three days before the fast. Stop drinking caffeine or soda and limit sugar intake during these days before the fast as well. You will be physically challenged enough on the first days of the fast, so you don't need a caffeine headache on top of that. Drinking lots of water in the days before the fast starts to help your body detoxify. If you are overweight, you may want to start cutting back before starting your fast. For example, maybe eat half portions for a few weeks before the fast.

If you are married, be sure your spouse is in agreement with you about the fast length and timing. It will affect your whole family so it is important to have them on board. Explain to your children what you are doing and why you are doing it. After the initial part of the fast you should be able to sit down with your family for dinner and still not eat. I even spend extra time cooking for my family when I am fasting because I just enjoy being around food, even though I am not tempted to eat it. One of my students Matt said this: "I started learning how to cook during the fast. I loved the smell of food…I ended up helping make dinner for about the last three weeks of the fast. A few times I made the entire dinner for my wife! I never had a desire to cook and now I am really getting into it. So funny."

If possible, plan extra times for prayer. Fasting is a distinct area of spiritual life, even when not combined with prayer. If you can withdraw and spend a lot of time in prayer, great! If not, understand that the fast itself is something of spiritual substance. As you might recall, the fast itself becomes a wordless prayer.

Get some spiritual accountability prayer from spiritual mentors, small group leaders, youth leaders or your pastor. Their prayers and spiritual covering are very important during the fast. If you are a minor, seek your parents permission. Spiritual covering, submission and unity are important factors when fasting. Ask these people if God is showing them anything about you. Get extra prayer as often as possible while on the fast.

During the fast

Often times the first part of the fast is difficult. As I mentioned previously you might get headaches and be grumpy. Franklin Hall explains it as poisons working loose in the body. After some days you get past this cleansing stage, hunger leaves and you generally don't get hungry anymore. This is an amazing experience. Habit hunger still comes sometimes at mealtimes, but you can be around food and not eat it, even if you are cooking as I mentioned. Once or twice I have struggled with hunger the whole way through a fast, but this is unusual for a long fast.

Hygiene is important. Jesus said in Matthew 6: 17-18, "But when you fast, put oil on your head and wash your face, so that it will not be obvious to others that you are fasting." For this reason, I tend to dress up more when I am fasting. Brushing your teeth two or three times a day is helpful. If you are not careful, your mouth odor could publicize your fast more than you intend.

Casual exercise is good. Going for walks is great. Absolutely avoid strenuous exercise after the first few days. Many times you will sleep lighter at night. This can be a great prayer time. You might find the need to take a nap during the day. After a week or two, you might experience some dizziness if you stand up rapidly. Pause or sit down and it will go away. This is normal. Sometimes there is pain and cramps in muscles; this is normal too. Depending on what you are eating and drinking it can affect your digestion, sometimes with embarrassing results. You will lose weight, about a pound a day on the water only fast. Thin people will lose less weight because they have less to lose.

One of things you will discover is that with your sense of taste dormant, your other senses might develop an increased capacity during the fast. You will notice things that other people don't. Often times when I am fasting I smell things that others around me do not. "Where is that smell of smoke coming from?" I might ask only to see blank stares. People around me don't smell it. Then I glance off in the distance and see smoke rising.

Despite the amazing results available from extended fasting, be aware that you will be opposed, especially during the first part of your fast. Prepare for opposition. On the day you start to fast don't be surprised if someone at your work or in your class brings a delicious snack to share. It should not be a surprise if you experience opposition from the enemy when fasting. Jesus did.

How to finish a fast

In order to maximize your fasting experience, you must end the fast slowly and carefully over several days. This is serious. You could end up in the hospital if you don't do it properly. Basically your digestive system shuts down and it can be dangerous if you eat too much too soon. Start with crackers and vegetable broth. Do not eat solid foods immediately after your fast. It is important to eat small amounts of easy-to-digest food every two to three hours for a few days. After thin soups, you can add milk, then yogurt, then raw salad, then boiled potatoes or bread every few hours.

Usually it is good to start to exercise mildly right away because this kickstarts your metabolism. As you gradually start to eat, start to gradually get mild exercise, increasing each time you do it.

A final thought is that you should not undertake another fast too soon. Your body needs time to recover. As a rule of thumb if you fast for twenty-one days, expect it to take twenty-one days for your body to fully recover from the fast.

What if you fail?

One of the people I learned fasting from tells the story that in the middle of an extended fast he messed up and ate a whole bag of potato chips. Did he quit the fast? No, he asked for forgiveness and continued the fast successfully. Another famous national leader in the USA said he failed on a fast and snuck some yogurt and chips. The next day one of his intercessors came to him and said, "I saw you in a dream. You were supposed to be fasting, but you were eating yogurt and chips." He took this as a good motivation to resume his fast where he left off.

If you fail, don't give in to condemnation and quit. God always extends grace. If you feel sick and weak, have someone pray for you. You don't have to make it all alone. If the Lord is inviting you to fast He will help you make it through.

1. Mike Bickle, *The Rewards of Fasting* (Kansas City, MI: Forerunner, 2005) Pg. 3
2. Dr. Zacharias Tannee Fomum, The Ministry of Fasting (New York, NY: Vantage, 1991) Pg. 46

Chapter Fourteen Questions

1. Why is it important to fast with specific areas of focus?

2. What is important to consider when preparing for a fast?

3. What is important to remember during the fast?

4. What should you consider as you end the fast?

CHAPTER FIFTEEN

The Invitation to Fast

> *Fasting is feasting on heavenly food. Daniel sought God with an undefiled diet and prayer and fasting. He had supernatural dreams and visions and supernatural understanding.[1] — Franklin Hall*

Can you feel the Lord inviting you to fast? Are you getting hungry for breakthroughs in your life? Are you getting hungry for spiritual growth? Are you getting hungry for the cleansing and humility that comes on an extended fast? I hope so. There are even times in the Bible where revelation of the future came when fasting. Daniel is a prime example of this.

But even as we recognize the many, dynamic benefits of fasting, it is important we keep it in proper perspective. It is not us trying to get something from God. It is not like a hunger strike, where we are demanding God do something for us.

Mike Bickle says it this way, "Fasting is more than denying ourselves food. It isn't really about getting hungry. While we do get hungry when we fast, fasting is really about experiencing more of God."[2] God is inviting you on fasting journey with Him. But you are not alone.

Will you join these Bible heroes?

Joel wrote to call the people back to God. "Declare a holy fast; call a sacred assembly. Summon the elders and all who live in the land to the house of the LORD your God, and cry out to the LORD" (Joel 1:14).

As I have mentioned before, Jehoshaphat set himself to seek the Lord in a time of trouble. He did not turn to man. He proclaimed a fast. His fast enabled him to humbly be honest with the Lord that they were not equal to their enemies. Fasting breaks the confidence in human effort, so for Jehoshaphat it was easy to cry out to the Lord for help when he did not know what to do. The Lord brought deliverance.

David was a man after God's own heart and his life was built around a thread of fasting. David even fasted for his enemies in Psalm 35:11. "Ruthless witnesses come forward; they question me on things I know nothing about. They repay me evil for good and leave me like one bereaved. Yet when they were ill, I put on sackcloth and humbled myself with fasting."

David was mocked and persecuted for fasting. Psalm 69:9-12 says, "...for zeal for your house consumes me, and the insults of those who insult you fall on me. When I weep and fast, I must endure scorn; when I put on sackcloth, people make sport of me. Those who sit at the gate mock me, and I am the song of the drunkards." It didn't matter to David. He wanted to please God.

Esther and other great women of the Bible fasted in times of crisis or need and saw the Lord come through. The Apostle Paul fasted the first three days of his Christian life, from the time the Lord Jesus appeared to him on the Damascus Road until his vision was restored when Ananias prayed for him. Later in writing to the Corinthians he identified fasting as a regular part of his leadership and ministry.

Will you join these historical figures?

Martin Luther was a man of exceptional courage and boldness. Because he fasted and prayed God moved through him in an extraordinary way. The message of justification by faith and by faith alone took hold of Germany and the rest of Europe and spread to all the earth.

John Knox was a man of fasting and prayer. His prayers were fueled by a life of fasting. He moved men and women to seek God. Queen Mary of Scotland said she feared the prayers of John Knox more than the whole army of the reigning monarch of England, Queen Elizabeth.

John Wesley saw clearly the importance of fasting and its necessity to ministry. He fasted twice a week all of his adult life. All who were preachers with him were required to fast twice a week as well. Wesley found it difficult to understand a Christian life that did not include fasting.

Jonathan Edwards possessed unquestionable spiritual power and authority. He was a man consecrated to the Lord and given to prayer and fasting. It is reported that he fasted so often it was sometimes difficult for him to maintain his balance while standing to preach. His fasting life was backed by his prayer life and his prayer life was sustained by his fasting life.

Charles Finney was totally yielded to the Lord and gave himself to fasting. He declared that each time he felt a reduction of the power of the Holy Spirit upon him he would withdraw for three days and nights of fasting. God always filled him with the power of the Holy Spirit after the fast. Because Finney discovered this secret and used it the anointing of the Holy Spirit was always upon him and he did great things for God. Businessmen, merchants, and men and women of high society were brought to the Lord through him. He firmly believed that fasting was one of the best methods to liberate the glorious power of the Holy Spirit.

Fasting to change a nation

Do you want to change a nation? John Piper documents the impact that fasting has had on the nation of Korea.

In the latter years of the twentieth century, fasting and prayer have almost become synonymous with the churches of South Korea. And there is good reason. The first Protestant church was planted in Korea in 1884. One hundred years later there were 30,000 churches. That is an average of 300 new churches a year for 100 years. At the end of the twentieth century, evangelicals comprise about 30% of the population. God has used many means to accomplish this great work. One of them is a recovery of not just dynamic prayer, but fasting prayer. For example, in the OMS (Overseas Missionary Society) churches alone more than 20,000 people have completed a forty-day fast, usually at one of their prayer houses at the mountains.[3]

Piper also writes of a day of prayer and fasting that saved the British from a French invasion in 1756. He is referring to what John Wesley wrote in his journal. The King of England called for a day of solemn prayer and fasting because of a threatened invasion of the French. Wesley wrote, "The fast day was a glorious day, such as London has scarce seen since the Restoration. Every church in the city was more than full, and a solemn, seriousness sat on every face. Surely God heareth prayer, and there will yet be a lengthening of our tranquility. The humility was turned into national rejoicing for the threatened invasion of the French was averted."[4]

Do you want your faith to grow?

Franklin Hall said that fasting is faith's greatest ally. Fasting increases your faith to believe things are possible that were not previously possible. The Bible talks about the gift of faith in 1 Corinthians 12:9, "...to another faith by the same Spirit." A simple definition of faith is to be fully convinced or persuaded about what is still unseen. While fasting a gift of faith can come for immediate needs to be met or for ongoing needs for the future.

Once while on a fast I was struggling with a need for a large amount of money for a project I was working on. I just couldn't see where this amount of money would come from. I was home alone and walking around our living room, praying about this project. I was about ready to decide we could not go ahead with it. As I sat down on the couch, all at once in an instant I received faith for this amount of money. It was so clear that I could still today tell you what couch I was sitting on and in what room of our house. I got up and set the project in motion and within a couple of months the money came from unexpected places to finish the project. A major part of the money came on day one of another forty-day fast. God did it.

When the "gift of faith" is in operation it takes you past present circumstances. "Now faith is being sure of what we hope for and certain of what we do not see" (Hebrews 11:1). Faith is increased by fasting which includes God encounters and humble obedience.

Larry Kreider says, "We starve our body in order to feed our spirit. The essence of a fast is self-denial in order to turn our thoughts to God....As we deny ourselves and focus on God, our faith deepens and becomes more powerful."[5]

The invitation

I believe the Lord might be inviting you to a life of fasting. As you consider this invitation, don't think of it as a religious "have to" but more as a personal invitation to join the Lord on a spiritual journey. What do you have to lose but a few pounds that are easily gained back? Who knows what God might do?

1. Franklin Hall, *The Fasting Prayer* (San Diego, CA: Self published, 1952) Pg. 47
2. Mike Bickle, *The Rewards of Fasting* (Kansas City, MI: Forerunner, 2005) Pg. 2
3. John Piper, *A Hunger for God* (Wheaton, IL: Crossway, 2013) Pg.96
4. Ibid Pg. 101
5. Larry Kreider, *Speak Lord I'm Listening* (Ventura, CA: Regal, 2008) Pg. 37

Chapter Fifteen Questions

1. Can you feel the Lord inviting you to fast? Are you getting hungry for breakthroughs and spiritual growth in your life? Are you getting hungry for the cleansing and humility that comes through an extended fast?

2. Discuss some leaders in the Bible who fasted and saw significant results.

3. Discuss some church leaders throughout history who lived a lifestyle of fasting.

4. Discuss people you know personally who have fasted and seen good fruit from it.

CHAPTER SIXTEEN

Who Knows?

> " Fasting is normal and basic to the Christian life—it is Christianity 101."[1] — Mike Bickle

I love the invitation and the possibility found in the story of Jonah. As we read what happened to Jonah in Nineveh, look for the words "Who knows?" When the King of Nineveh says these words, he opens up the door of possibility. Who knows what God might do?

Then the word of the Lord came to Jonah a second time: "Go to the great city of Nineveh and proclaim to it the message I give you." Jonah obeyed the word of the Lord and went to Nineveh. Now Nineveh was a very large city; it took three days to go through it. Jonah began by going a day's journey into the city, proclaiming, "Forty more days and Nineveh will be overthrown." The Ninevites believed God. A fast was proclaimed, and all of them, from the greatest to the least, put on sackcloth.

When Jonah's warning reached the king of Nineveh, he rose from his throne, took off his royal robes, covered himself with sackcloth and sat down in the dust. This is the proclamation he issued in Nineveh: "By the decree of the king and his nobles: Do not let people or animals, herds or flocks, taste anything; do not let them eat or drink. But let people and animals be covered with sackcloth. Let everyone call urgently on God. Let them give up their evil ways and their violence. **Who knows?** God may yet relent and with compassion turn from his fierce anger so that we will not perish" (Jonah 3:1-9).

Who knows? God might relent and have compassion. In the case of Ninevah, He did. Wasn't Nineveh destined for destruction? Yes, but the Ninevites believed God's warning and called for a fast. The king himself proclaimed that none should eat or drink, not even the animals. They should all call on the Lord and repent of their evil ways. They did exactly that and God spared them.

Did God change his mind? Some people would read this and say God changed His mind. But from God's point of view, He never changes His mind and His nature never changes. However, man can be given alternative outcomes that depend on what they do. God's promises are conditional based on the actions of man. Promises of blessings are conditional on the response of the one who receives them.

Having said that, let's return to the possibilities created when we hear the question inviting us to fast, "Who knows?"

Who knows what God might do if we turn to Him with prayer and fasting? Amazingly the same two possibility-filled words are found when Joel is talking about fasting.

> Rend your heart and not your garments. Return to the Lord your God, for he is gracious and compassionate, slow to anger and abounding in love, and he relents from sending calamity. **Who knows?** He may turn and relent and leave behind a blessing—grain offerings and drink offerings for the Lord your God (Joel 2: 13-14).

Who knows? Who knows what is possible? Who knows what might change? Who knows what God might do in our family, our city or our nation? I guess we don't know if we don't try. We know from the Scriptures that God is prepared to show mercy whenever people repent with fasting, regardless how horrible their past record has been.

Fasting moves God. He finds it difficult to turn a deaf ear to the fasting believer. It is true that God speaks to those who are listening, but my experience is that God speaks more to those who are listening and fasting. Or maybe fasting increases our ability to hear what God is saying.

Take a risk

Could you be disappointed if you engage God through prayer and fasting? There is always that possibility. My times of fasting have always been powerful, but not always easy. Don't expect it to be easy. Look at what happened to Moses. He spent forty days fasting and experiencing the glory of

God at the top of the mountain. He was physically hidden by the tangible glory of God. But when he came down from the mountain the situation on the ground had changed and the people were worshiping an idol. He got angry and threw down the tablets containing the law of God written by the very finger of God.

Yes, there is risk. But there is also the possibility of great reward. Take note of this quote from Dr. Fomum: "Sometimes it will seem like those who do not fast and pray are more successful in ministry than the one who is wrestling with principalities and powers through fasting. Remember, it may take days, weeks, or months to catch a whale. Deep sea fisherman do not catch as many fish as surface fishermen, but when they do have a catch it is worth all the waiting and the struggling."[2] It is sacrifice now for a greater reward to come later. Delayed gratification.

I believe in fasting so much. This testimony is from another young person whom I have taught the principles in this book. This is how Matt describes his fasting experience:

> The longest I have ever fasted was eight days until this time. I was seeking God one morning and praying into a prophetic word I received months prior. The Lord very clearly told me to fast for forty days on clear juices only. There was an immediate "yes" from me with no hesitation. I don't know how else to explain the clarity in my mind other than saying that I wanted to do it and it just made perfect sense. Truly when God speaks

His grace is immediately deposited to the willing heart to do what He has commanded. I called my wife and told her what happened. She agreed, so I began the fast right then. The encounters I had with the Lord on this fast were intimate and incredible. There was so much deposited into me regarding the specific things I was seeking God for—far more than I could have asked or even imagined. My life has truly been marked by God in a deeper way during this fast!

In this book I have attempted to persuade you that you can fast, see amazing growth in your relationship with God and see many breakthroughs for you own life and others. Even if you have never fasted a day in your life, you can start now. Even as I am writing these closing words I sense the Lord calling me to start a fast in the next few days. Who knows what the Lord might do?

AUTHORS NOTE: Not everyone should fast from physical food. Some physical conditions require food and you would harm yourself if you do not eat. God would not have you harm yourself physically. Before attempting extended fasting, please consult your physician.

1. Mike Bickle, *The Rewards of Fasting* (Kansas City, MI: Forerunner, 2005) Pg. 1
2. Dr. Zacharias Tannee Fomum, The Ministry of Fasting (New York, NY: Vantage, 1991) Pg. 233

Chapter Sixteen Questions

1. Explain what Mike Bickle means when he says, "Fasting is normal and basic to the Christian Life – It is Christianity 101."

2. Why is there risk involved when going on an extended fast?

3. Why do you think the Bible includes the example of the pagan King of Nineveh calling for a fast?

4. If the impossible becomes possible while fasting what is holding you back from fasting?

Twenty Practical Suggestions for the Extended Fast

1. **Start gradually with shorter lengths of time.** Don't start with forty days. Three or seven days is a good warm-up.

2. **Look for spiritual accountability** from a small group leader, pastor or youth leader. Their prayers and spiritual covering are very important during fasting.

3. **If you have any concerns and/or medical conditions**, consult a doctor before starting an extended fast.

4. **If you are overweight**, you may want to cut back on food before starting your fast. For example, eat half portions for a few weeks before the fast.

5. **Don't weigh yourself.** This makes it seem like a diet instead of a fast. You will lose weight, about a pound a day on the water only fast. Thin people will lose less weight.

6. **If you are married, be sure your spouse is in agreement** about the fast length and timing. Your fast will affect your whole family.

7. **Fasting is a distinct area of spiritual life, even when not combined with prayer.** If you can withdraw and spend a lot of time in prayer, great. If not, understand that the fast itself is something of spiritual substance. The fast becomes a prayer.

8. **If you are working on a job that involves heavy physical labor, drink juice during your fast.** Franklin Hall suggested a three-day complete fast and then five hundred calories a day in juices for the forty-day duration. Dilute acidic juices like orange or tomato juice.

9. **Ease into your fast.** Cut back to eating only fruit, vegetables and simple foods for three days before the fast. Stop caffeine and sugar intake during these days before the fast.

10. **Often times the first part of the fast is difficult.** You may get headaches and be grumpy. This is part of the fleshly desires coming to the surface for elimination. Hunger usually leaves after four to six days. Don't be surprised if you experience opposition from the enemy; Jesus did.

11. **Brush your teeth two or three times a day.** The mouth odor could publicize your fast.

12. **Casual exercise such as going for walks is good.** Absolutely avoid strenuous exercise after the first few days.

13. **You may sleep lighter at night.** This can be a great prayer time. You might find the need to take a nap during the day.

14. **You may develop an increased capacity to taste and smell** during the fast.

15. **You may experience dizziness if you stand up rapidly** after a week or two. Pause or sit down and it will go away. This is normal.

16. **END YOUR FAST GRADUALLY.** The fast must be broken very carefully. Start with juice and vegetable broth. Do not eat solid foods immediately after your fast. It is important to eat small

amounts of easy-to-digest food every two to three hours for a few days. After juices, then start thin soups, then milk or yogurt, then raw salad, boiled potatoes or bread every few hours.

17. **Journal your fasting experience.** When the fast is over, write down the results and what you have heard from God. Evaluate decisions you made during fasting.

18. **Most of the time, results will be seen during the fast.** However, the greatest results tend to be in the weeks, months and years following completion of the fast. A lot is happening that can't be seen or felt.

19. **A complete fast is defined as a fast with only drinking water.**

20. **An absolute fast is defined as a fast with no food or water.** An absolute fast should be no longer than three days.

APPENDIX B

Forty Reasons
Why We Should Fast

By Rev. Franklin Hall

1. Perhaps the main reason why we should fast is because Jesus, our Redeemer, placed a fast upon all of us. Matthew 9:15 says, "And Jesus said unto them, Can the children of the bride-chamber mourn, as long as the bridegroom is with them? But the days will come, when the bridegroom shall be taken from them, then shall they fast." We therefore are to fast to carry on the works for the kingdom that Jesus started by His fastings and prayers.

2. We should fast because fasting was a part and parcel of the life of our Lord, Jesus Christ (Matthew 4:1,2; John 6:27) and He urged us to follow Him (Luke 9:23).

3. Jesus taught fasting as one of the four foundations of the Christian faith. These foundations are: giving, praying, fasting and faith. (Please study Matthew 6).

4. Paul was "in fastings often" (2 Corinthians. 11:27). He instructed us to be "…approving ourselves as the ministers of God (among other things) …in fastings" (2 Corinthians 6:5).

5. Every single person in the early church fasted (Acts 14:23). We therefore are not to do less.

6. Fasting enables one to become a conductor of spiritual power for either blessing others or for bringing blessing to himself.

7. Proper fasting with sincerity and respect to the Lord will positively break the yokes of sin, sickness and spiritual oppression (Isaiah 58:6).

8. Fasting becomes prayer to the praying Christian. When unable to pray (like David), it enables one to be so anointed that prayer reaches through to God. Psalm 35:13: "I humbled my soul with fasting and my prayer returned unto my bosom."

9. Fasting intensifies the power of prayer many times so that even short prayers bring results.

10. Fasting reaches and obtains what prayer alone cannot, because it removes unbelief (Matthew 17:20, 21).

11. Fasting brings one into direct contact with unbelief, so that it can be removed. Unbelief can never be fully apprehended until one fasts from ten to forty days.

12. Fasting is the greatest faith producer because the fasting and the faith organ are one and the same-the mouth organ (Romans 10:9, 10).

13. Fasting is more closely related to faith than any other Christian work, and in fact is the very gateway to trust and have faith in God after conversion. However, because it is little taught about and understood, folk fail to realize its value. (Here we are dealing with consecrated fasting).

14. Fasting will bring about word-faith power (Luke. 4:2, 32, 36). Jesus' "word" was not "with power" until after His fast.

15. Fasting will blitzkrieg the devil. (Author's note: blitzkrieg is a German term for "lightning war," a military tactic that creates disorganization among enemy forces through intense, fast, powerful attacks; it is intended to bring about a swift victory.)

16. Fasting masters the old man, subjugating the flesh (1 Corinthians 9:27), and is mortification of the flesh and members (Colossians 3:5).

17. Fasting pleases the Spirit. The flesh and the Spirit are at enmity with each other.

18. Fasting is the most sure spiritual method to bring a revival. A revival begins in our heart first, then one comes about in the community. Souls become saved.

19. Fasting enables one to transcend the natural and takes one quickly into the spiritual realm. We may become so personal and intimate with Jesus that we smell His body. He is a sweet smelling savor.

20. Fasting brings one nearer to Christ than any other known process. It enables one to become clothed with the full Baptism of the Holy Ghost and with Fire. (Please see Exodus 14; 34:27-35; Deuteronomy 34:7; Isaiah 58:1-10; 60:1-5, 21, 23; 61:10; Matthew. 3:11, 12.)

21. There is more judgment pronounced upon those given to food addiction than to alcoholic drunkards (in the Bible). Sin is sin whether it comes under the good name of "food" or under some more insidious term. (Please study Numbers 11: 9-34; Psalm 78; Matthew 24:38; Luke. 21:34; and Romans 16:17, 18.) Most Christians are unknowingly bound to the sin of "habit hunger" (actually, food addiction). A protracted fast will break this yoke in as little as three days' time, and will keep an individual free with temperate eating.

22. Fasting will undo all sins of intemperance (after Jesus' blood has first washed away our sins).

23. Fasting will crucify the flesh and all unnatural desires associated with lusts of any appetite gratification.

24. Fasting can be self-chastisement and will prevent many chastisements of the Lord from coming upon us (1 Kings 21:25-29; Jonah 3: 5-10).

25. Fasting is the easiest way for backsliders to come home. (Study David's fasts.) Refer to Psalms 35:13; 109:24.

26. Fasting places our natural appetites into a dormant condition, thus physical pleasures are not enjoyed while our flesh becomes sublimated. With pleasurable appetites static, God can come near us and we near Him.

27. Fasting thus changes one's environment from the natural to the spiritual. A revival comes about inside us, along with the proper burdens that we should carry for others.

28. Fasting will change a life of defeat into one of victory and will bring healing and new life to both body and soul.

29. Fasting, when properly entered into, is the surest method of consecration and sanctification.

30. Fasting develops the fruit of the Spirit and enables one to grow into maturity, with matured fruit.

31. Proper fasting will help one to receive spiritual gifts. Most Christians, like the children of Israel, are wasting forty years of their lifetime (even with speaking in tongues) without deeper spiritual gift manifestations and without the fruit of the Spirit, just because they fail to fast as they should. (Please study Deuteronomy 8:2, 3; Daniel 1:3-17.)

32. Fasting consumes and burns out the very roots of fleshly lusts.

33. Fasting brings one into the misery and sufferings of the fleshly nature in such a manner that he can see himself in the same light that Jesus sees him. He realizes his nakedness (Revelation 3:17) so he begins to be clothed with power, receiving the more complete baptism into the Holy Ghost healing fire.

34. Fasting gives the child of God spiritual manifestations in a tangible manner. The absence of the natural menu prepares his appetite for the "hidden (supernatural) manna" (John 4:32, 34; 6:27-58; Revelation 2:17).

35. Fasting always brings revelations and better understanding. Sometimes visions and unspeakable glory will be attained and manifested (Daniel 10:2-21; Acts 10: 9-16).

36. Fasting will always enable one to obtain the direction and anointing needed for the work to which he is called.

37. Fasting enlarges our capacity. Many of us have only a thimble-size capacity. We might be full at times, but how full? Shouting and spiritual emotion do not always indicate how large our capacities are. A person may be running over with only a thimble-size capacity. Fasting will give a well-size or even unlimited capacity to enjoy the riches of heaven, immortality, glory, honor, and power. (Refer to John 3:34; Ephesians 4:13).

38. Fasting and its related terms of expression are mentioned one third as many times in the Bible as prayer. To every two sermons you hear preached on prayer, you should hear a third on fasting. The author asks the reader this question: How many times has he ever heard a sermon on fasting in his lifetime? It is truly deplorable that such a major doctrine in both Old and New Testaments has been so neglected, ignored, and disrespected.

39. The Lord places a definite fast on the children of Israel (Deuteronomy 6:11, 12; 8:3, 12-14, etc.) in order that their unbelief environment, acquired in the land of Egypt, could be broken, and they could more speedily enter the promised land. Because they rejected these fastings their few days journey was drawn out to forty years. We should take heed to this sad lesson and hasten to fast, so we may enter into the promises the Lord has waiting for us (John 11:24-26; 2 Timothy 1:10; 1 John 2:25).

40. Jesus is pleased when we come to Him in this consecrated manner. As we free ourselves from the natural we exalt Him to the highest. Don't worry, you will be rewarded a thousand times.

APPENDIX C

The Daniel Fast

The concept of a Daniel fast comes from Daniel 1:8-14,

> "But Daniel resolved not to defile himself with the royal food and wine, and he asked the chief official for permission not to defile himself this way. Now God had caused the official to show favor and sympathy to Daniel, but the official told Daniel, "I am afraid of my lord the king, who has assigned your food and drink. Why should he see you looking worse than the other young men your age? The king would then have my head because of you." Daniel then said to the guard whom the chief official had appointed over Daniel, Hananiah, Mishael and Azariah, "Please test your servants for ten days: Give us nothing but vegetables to eat and water to drink. Then compare our appearance with that of the young men who eat the royal food, and treat your servants in accordance with what you see." So he agreed to this and tested them for ten days."

The background of the "Daniel fast" is that Daniel and his three friends had been "deported" to Babylon when Nebuchadnezzar and the Babylonians had conquered Judah (2 Kings 24:13-14). Daniel and his three friends were put into the Babylonian court servant "training program." Part of the program was learning Babylonian customs, beliefs, laws, and practices. The eating habits of the Babylonians were not in complete agreement with the Mosaic law. As a result, Daniel asked if he and his three friends could be excused from eating the meat (which was likely sacrificed to Babylonian false gods and idols).

A Daniel fast is eating only fruits and vegetables for a certain amount of time, abstaining from meat products. Some people use a Daniel fast as a dieting method. Some use a Daniel fast instead of fasting from food entirely. The Bible nowhere commands believers to observe a Daniel fast. As a result, it is a matter of Christian freedom whether to observe a Daniel fast. The fast can last as long as you want. Unless God has called you to fast, then you should fast as long as He wants. Understand that fasting is a very personal thing between you and God. Be sure to make time to pray to become closer to Him.

Yield all results to God. Daniel said, "as you see fit, deal with your servants" (Daniel 1:13). The Daniel fast will lead to spiritual insight. "to those four young men God gave knowledge." The Daniel fast is longer than one day. These young men fasted for ten days. The Daniel Fast is a partial fast. They ate, but only vegetables and water. The Daniel Fast requires abstinence from party or junk foods. There is no indication that they ever began to eat the king's food.

You may experience moderate to severe headaches for the first day or two as your body rids itself of caffeine, salt, sugar, and various impurities. You may need to take a pain-killer or aspirin.

IMPORTANT EXCEPTIONS: Anyone with a medical condition related to eating or under the treatment of a physician must consult their doctor. Children, especially small children, will have special needs that must be considered. Under these conditions, find some sacrifice in the area of food that can be made without endangering health. Also, if you have extreme difficulty with the fast, such as impairment of your ability to work at your job, you will have to make adjustments. This is not a failure of will but is wisdom. Seek the Lord and discuss it with other Christians involved in the fast to find alternatives.

Information sourced from *www.gotquestions.org*

Guidelines
for the Daniel Fast

Daniel Fast - Foods to Include

- **All fruits**. Fresh, frozen, dried, juiced or canned including apples, apricots, bananas, blackberries, blueberries, cantaloupe, cherries, figs, grapefruit, grapes, honeydew melon, kiwi, lemons, limes, nectarines, oranges, peaches, pears, pineapples, plums, prunes, raisins, raspberries, strawberries, watermelon.

- **All vegetables**. Fresh, frozen, dried, juiced or canned including artichokes, asparagus, beets, broccoli, Brussels sprouts, cabbage, carrots, cauliflower, celery, chili peppers, collard greens, corn, cucumbers, eggplant, garlic, kale, lettuce, mushrooms, mustard greens, okra, onions, potatoes, radishes, spinach, squashes, sweet potatoes, tomatoes, turnips, watercress, yams, zucchini, veggie burgers.

- **All whole grains,** including whole wheat, brown rice, millet, quinoa, oats, barley, grits, whole wheat pasta, whole wheat tortillas, rice cakes and popcorn.

- **All nuts and seeds**, including sunflower seeds, cashews, peanuts, sesame...also nut butters (peanut butter).

- **All legumes**. Canned or dried beans, pinto beans, lentils, black eyed peas, kidney beans, black beans.

- **All quality oils** including olive, canola, grape seed, peanut, and sesame.

- **Beverages** spring water, distilled water or other pure waters, juice. Drink eight glasses of water daily throughout the fast. This is very important.

- **Other** tofu, soy products, vinegar, seasonings, salt, herbs and spices.

Daniel Fast - Foods to Avoid

- **All meat and animal products** including beef, lamb, pork, poultry, and fish.

- **All dairy products** including milk, cheese, cream, butter, and eggs.

- **All sweeteners** including sugar, raw sugar, honey, syrups, and molasses.

- **All leavened bread** including Ezekiel Bread (it contains yeast and honey) and baked goods.

- **All refined, processed foods.** Artificial flavorings, food additives, preservatives, white rice and flour.

- **All deep fried foods** including potato chips, French fries, corn chips.

- **All solid fats** including shortening, margarine, lard and foods high in fat.

- **Beverages** including coffee, tea, herbal teas, carbonated beverages, energy drinks and alcohol.

Recommended Reading

Mike Bickle, *The Rewards of Fasting* (Kansas City, MI: Forerunner, 2005)

Bill Bright, *The Coming Revival* (Orlando, FL: New Life, 1995)

Mahesh Chavda, *The Hidden Power of Prayer and Fasting* (Shippensburg, PA: Destiny Image, 1998)

Dr. Zacharias Tannee Fomum, *The Ministry of Fasting* (New York, NY: Vantage, 1991)

Jentezen Franklin, *Fasting* (Lake Mary, FL: Charisma House, 2008)

Franklin Hall, *Atomic Power with God Thru Fasting and Prayer* (San Diego, CA: Self published, 1952)

Larry Kreider, *Speak Lord I'm Listening* (Ventura, CA: Regal, 2008)

Mark Owan, *No Easy Day* (New York, NY: Penguin Group, 2014)

John Piper, *A Hunger for God* (Wheaton, IL: Crossway, 2013)

Elmer L Towns, *Fasting for Financial Breakthrough* (Ventura, CA: Regal, 2002)

Elmer L. Towns, *Fasting for Spiritual Breakthrough* (Ventura, CA: Regal, 1996)

Other books by Brian Sauder

A Practical Path to a Prosperous Life

A clear biblical, step-by-step approach to attaining abundant personal finances, building wealth and financing of the Great Commission in our day. Brian draws on age-old biblical truths and includes many practical, present-day applications to help your thinking line up with the God's Word. Brian's dream is to help identify and eradicate the poverty mindset from the church so that every believer is empowered to experience God's abundance and to fulfill his or her destiny. 282 pages **$12.99**

Biblical Role of Elders for Today's Church

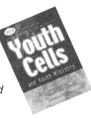

New Testament leadership principles for equipping elders. Learn what elders' qualifications and responsibilities are, how elders are chosen, how they can be spiritual fathers and mothers, resolve conflicts, and more. *by Larry Kreider, Ron Myer, Steve Prokopchak, Brian Sauder. 278 pages.* **$12.99**

Youth Cells and Youth Ministry

God's heart is expressed for the postmodern generations in the relationship and trust that is provided by youth cell groups. Small groups are a safe place to learn, discuss, cry, get healed, develop gifts and reach out. This book gives revealing insights into today's youth culture, along with the specifics of implementing cell ministry. *by Brian Sauder and Sarah Mohler 120 pages.* **$8.50**

Helping You Build Cell Churches

This complete biblical blueprint for small group ministry covers 54 topics! It gives full, integrated training to build cell churches from the ground up. *Compiled by Brian Sauder and Larry Kreider, 224 pages.* **$19.95**

For more resources, seminar details and to order visit www.dcfi.org
call 1.800.848.5892   Email: info@dcfi.org

Brian Sauder currently serves on the International Apostolic Council of DOVE International. He also directs the DOVE Training Schools, which are now available in an online format. Brian helps to provide oversight and direction for DOVE churches in Canada, USA, India and South Africa. Brian and his wife, Janet, have over thirty years of experience in leadership of churches, small groups, youth groups, government and business.

Initially trained as an Industrial Engineer at Penn State University, Brian now provides others with the tools to design and build churches, ministries and organizations. In 2017 Brian completed a Masters of Organizational Leadership at Regent University. Much of his time is spent traveling to oversee churches and coaching leaders in leadership development. Brian served nine years as an elected government official on the local public school board including two years as board president.

Brian is the author of the book *A Practical Path to a Prosperous Life* that was birthed out of a personal revelation which has since become a life message. He is co-author of the book *The Biblical Role of Elders*. He also compiled *Helping You Build Cell Churches*, a training manual for pastors, small group leaders and church planters.

Brian and Janet have five children and have been married for over thirty years. They reside in Manheim, Pennsylvania.

Visit Brian's blog at futurenhope.com

Made in the
USA
Middletown, DE